Islam

Markus Hattstein

Islam

Religion and Culture

KÖNEMANN

The Origin of Islam

Islam means submission to God. The youngest of the world religions professes its faith in Allah, the One God, and thus embodies an uncompromising monotheism. In his native city of Mecca, where he continued to encourage the people to lead a God-fearing and socially responsible life, Prophet Muhammad, the Messenger of God, first announced the divine revelations that had been made to him. Forced to depart for Medina in 622 CE (Common Era, see page 95) as a result of growing opposition, the Prophet was transformed into the political leader of a rapidly growing community. This year, known as The Hijrah, marks the beginning of the Islamic calendar. In 630 CE he captured Mecca and reclaimed the city's *Ka'bah*, with its Black Stone, as the central shrine of the Muslims.

God's message, as revealed directly to Muhammad, is written down in the Qur'an, the holy book of Islam. The *hadiths*, a record of the Prophet's words and deeds, represent Islam's secondary written authority.

Mount Hira, 17th century
Persian miniature

*Recite in the
Name of God,
The Compassionate,
The Merciful.*

*Recite in the name of
your Lord who
created—created
man from clots of
blood.*

*Recite! Your Lord is
the Most Bountiful
One, who by the pen
taught man what he
did not know.*

*Indeed, man
transgresses in
thinking himself his
own master: for to
your Lord all things
return.*

Sura 96, 1–9 (the
oldest sura in the
Qur'an)

Opposite:
**Muhammad and Ali
cleanse the *Ka'bah*
of idols**, 1585–1595
Miniature from the
Raudat as-Safa of Mir
Havand, Shiraz, Iran

**Muhammad, Ali and
Fatima,** 18th century
Turkish miniature,
Istanbul, Museum
of Turkish and
Islamic art

Muhammad and the Revelation of God

Muhammad was born in Mecca into the Quraysh tribe around 570 CE. His father died before his birth, and his mother when he was six. After her death he was initially brought up by his grandfather and subsequently by his respected uncle, Abu Talib, who then protected Muhammad right up to his own death. At the age of about 25, Muhammad married Khadijah, who was older than him. She was the prosperous widow of a merchant, whose caravans he drove. He remained devoted to her until the end of her life, 25 years later. Together they had two sons, who did not survive childhood, and four daughters.

Medina at the time of the Prophet, 1798 Turkish miniature, Dublin, Chester Beatty Library

From the time of his departure from Mecca, Medina became the home of the Prophet and his followers, and his house served as the meeting place of the rapidly growing community. Fierce competition between Medina and Mecca, meant Muhammad's skills as a mediator were required to reconcile his different supporters. His burial mosque was splendidly decorated by the Ottomans, although the strict Wahhabis still forbid any cult of his tomb.

Saudi Arabian landscape

The Prophet's native land, current-day Saudi Arabia, is 99 percent covered by desert and desert steppe, and has a dry and hot climate. Its culture was governed by the lifestyles of the nomads with their clans and caravans. Muhammad, who was also a trader, succeeded to a large extent in uniting the rival nomadic tribes.

At the time of Muhammad's birth, the Arabian Peninsula was still largely dominated by polytheism. For the most part, its different gods were identified with the stars or had some regional significance, such as Hubal, who was worshipped in Mecca. At the same time, however, monotheism was attracting a growing number of followers. These supporters were already speaking of the One God as "the God," *al-ilah*, which was contracted to "Allah." It is probable that Muhammad first came into contact with Judaism and Christianity on his travels with the caravan, which took him to northern Arabia and Syria.

In 610 CE, on Mount Hira, Muhammad experienced his first revelation, which is dramatically described in Sura 96, the oldest of the Qur'anic suras. Archangel Gabriel came to him with a book and commanded him to "Read!" or "Recite!" Gabriel then announced that Muhammad was the Messenger of God. Following a period of inner doubt and despondency, he accepted the revelations and resolutely embraced his calling as prophet. During this time in and around Mecca his preaching concentrated not only on his experience of being called upon by God and on the real significance of the traditional revealed religions, but also told of the importance of divine judgment. Muhammad preached against the dangers of religious and social indifference in the community, and professed an increasingly radical monotheism. This led to a direct conflict with the Meccans, who profited from the pilgrimages to the city's ancient Arabian polytheistic shrine. Muhammad, on the other hand, embraced the Hanif tradition of the Arabian seekers after One God, who, in their hatred of polytheism, devoted themselves to the search.

Following the deaths of his uncle, Abu Talib, and his wife, Khadijah, in 619 CE, the socially isolated position of Muhammad and his followers became increasingly difficult as their conflict with the people of Mecca intensified. A proportion of his followers had emigrated to Abyssinia in 615 CE, so, in 622 CE, the Prophet departed from Mecca with the remainder for Yathrib, later Medina (from *madinat an-nabi*, meaning "the city of the Prophet"). He had previously received an invitation from leaders in Hathrib to come and arbitrate in various disputes. This "emigration" (*Hegira*) marks the beginning of the Islamic calendar and the *de facto* birth of the Islamic community (*Ummah*).

From Prophet to Politician

In Medina, Muhammad underwent a transformation from prophet and admonitory preacher to farsighted statesman and organizer of the young Islamic body. He was impressed by the large Jewish community there and adopted many of the rules of their religious life, such as ritual fasting. He also declared Abraham to have been a prototype Muslim, a model of the monotheistic seeker of God and a prophet, as well as the builder of the *Ka'bah* in Mecca. As he considered himself to be responsible for the restoration of monotheistic revealed religion, Muhammad at first believed that acceptance of the new religion would present no great difficulty to the Jews. When this proved not to be the case he took action against them, forcing large numbers of them to emigrate, and in 624 CE changed the direction of prayer from Jerusalem to that of Mecca. However, Jerusalem remained an important point of reference for Islam, mainly due to the story of the Prophet's night journey to heaven from Jerusalem on his mount, Buraq. After Mecca and Medina, Jerusalem is Islam's third holy city. Muhammad consolidated his ever-growing community, which was being joined by increasing numbers of the region's tribes, by drawing up an early system of government and settling with great skill traditional conflicts between his

various groups of followers. He managed to generate a vital sense of unity and identity by winning his Arab adherents away from their hitherto tribal and clan orientation to a common religion and the unity of belief in the One God. He also succeeded in moderating the ancient Arabian blood feud customs. Muhammad's prime political goal was his battle against the non-believing Meccans, which led—with

Muhammad and his followers march on Mecca, second half of the 16th century Miniature from the *Siyer-i Nabi,* Istanbul

In 630 CE the Prophet captured his native city of Mecca without resistance. He was able to win many new followers by showing clemency to his enemies.

Muhammad preaching to his followers
Turkish miniature

Muhammad's earliest preaching in Mecca tells of the goodness and omnipotence of God. Muhammad also spoke of his divine calling, urged his listeners to turn away from the worldly pursuit of profit and instead exercise generosity toward their fellow men, and exhorted mankind to profess faith in One God, Allah.

Muhammad continued to live in Medina, where he received tribal leaders from all over Arabia, who came to announce the conversion of their tribes to Islam. In 632 CE he undertook his final pilgrimage to Mecca, which was to become the precursor of the present-day pilgrimage (*Hajj*) undertaken by Muslims. Having already achieved the spread of Islam throughout most of the Arabian Peninsula, Muhammad was contemplating plans for the conquest of Byzantium and Persia when he died in his house in Medina on June 8, 632 CE, following a short illness.

varying results—to attacks on caravans and full-blown battles in which he proved himself to be a talented military leader. In 624 CE he defeated a Meccan force ten times the size of his own in the Battle of Badr. Soon afterwards he suffered a severe defeat, although this in turn was followed by a magnificent victory in 627 CE in what became known as the War of the Trench. In 628 CE he agreed a cease-fire with the Meccan forces, but two years later marched on his native city with 10,000 of his followers and was able to take it without encountering any significant resistance. As a result of his merciful treatment of his former enemies he was quickly able to win them over. Shortly afterwards he was able to set about cleansing the *Ka'bah* of idols, turning the Meccan's ancient Arabian shrine into one that was exclusively monotheistic and dedicated to the worship of One God, Allah.

Muhammad's night journey to heaven on his mount Buraq
1458
Persian miniature, Istanbul, Museum for Turkish and Islamic Art

The Prophet's night journey to heaven, described in detail in Sura 17, during which God took him from Mecca to Jerusalem and back, has always been a favorite subject of Islamic miniature painters. In particular, it is Muhammad's centaur-like mount, Buraq, with his human head, that has repeatedly captured the imagination of artists.

The Qur'an and the *Hadiths*

The Qur'an (from *qur'an*, meaning "reading, lecture"), the sacred book of Islam, is held to be God's Revelation as transmitted word for word to the Prophet Muhammad. It comprises 114 sections (suras) of varying length, which originated during the different phases of Muhammad's work. It is considered to fall into three Meccan phases (whose language is characterized by short prophetic and poetic formulas and the use of oaths), and a Medina phase (whose tone is fuller and more instructive and frequently deals with the everyday problems encountered by the young Islamic community).
With the exception of Sura 1, which takes the form of a prayer, the suras are arranged in decreasing length; thus Sura 2 has 286 verses while the closing suras only have three to five. They are not complete units in themselves nor arranged in the order in which they originated, but mostly contain fragments

Page of the Qur'an from Tunisia, beginning of the 10th century
Paris, Institut du monde arabe

of texts from different periods. The order used today goes back to the third caliph, Uthman (644–656 CE). All the suras have names that feature a characteristic word or theme that appears in them, and all except Sura 9 begin with the *basmala*, the invocation "In the Name of God, the Compassionate, the Merciful."
The original language of the Qur'an's rhyming prose was classical Arabic, which has been regarded as the religious language of all Muslims ever since. As Muslims view the Qur'an as a word-for-word rendering of the revelations made to Muhammad, for a long time it was a matter for debate whether it could be translated into other languages at all. Another dispute concerned the origins of the Qur'an. The Mutazilites, in order to emphasize the unity and

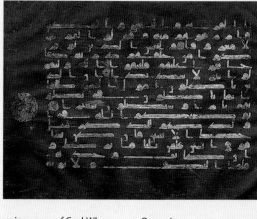

uniqueness of God, Who was all that existed in the beginning, considered it to have been "created," while with the current Asharite orthodoxy, the view has come to predominate that the Qur'an in its original form has existed as the "Word of God" since the very beginning of time. It is important for Muslims not simply to have a good knowledge of the Qur'an, but also to be able to recite it perfectly, and this is taught as a discipline in its own right. Speaking tempo and emphasis are particularly important. There are innumerable occasions in the life of Muslims that call for recitation of the Qur'an. The *hadiths* (from the Arabic *hadith*, meaning

Page from an Almohad Qur'an, end of the 12th century

Opposite:
Suras from the Qur'an, 1389
Arabic illuminated manuscript
Munich, Bavarian State Library

"announcement") are regarded as the religion's second most important authority, and Islamic law is based on both sources. The *hadiths* are the handed-down accounts of the deeds and sayings of the Prophet. Today, the majority of Muslims recognize six *hadith* collections as authentic. An important criterion is the unbroken chain of those passing on the tradition right back to Muhammad and his closest associates. The Shiites also recognize as *hadiths* the traditions that originated with Ali and the imams (community prayer leaders) who succeeded him.

The Basis of Faith

Islam has a special relationship with Judaism and Christianity. Not only are Moses and Jesus highly revered as prophets, but also Jews and Christians, as People of the Book, are given special rights of protection under Muslim rule. Further, the Islamic conception of God and man also reveals many similarities with these other two religions.

Although (like other religions) Islam adheres to its claim of being the one true faith, it generally adopts a pragmatic attitude in its dealings with other religions. However, any form of polytheism is regarded as the gravest of sins.

Islam emphasizes the importance of practicing the faith in accordance with the Five Pillars of Islam—profession of one's faith, ritual prayer, the giving of alms or payment of dues, fasting, and the pilgrimage to Mecca. In addition to the Five Pillars, the social structure of Islam is also supported by a series of religious holidays. Ritual prayer is performed primarily in the mosque, the Islamic place of worship.

Guardian angels recording the deeds of men in their scrolls, 1280
Miniature from *The Wonders of Creation,* Wasit, Iraq

A Bedouin came to the Prophet and said: "Tell me of such a deed as will make me enter Paradise, if I do it." The Prophet said: "Worship Allah, and worship none along with Him, offer the prescribed compulsory prayers perfectly, pay the compulsory Zakat, and fast the month of Ramadan." The Bedouin said: "By Him in whose hands my life is, I will not do more than this." When he (the Bedouin) left, the Prophet said: "Whoever likes to see a man of Paradise, then he may look at this man."

Hadith narrated by Abu Huraira

Opposite:
Man at prayer in a mosque

Pilgrims in Mecca, Saudi Arabia
Photograph taken 1976

Islam, Judaism and Christianity

Islam refers a great deal to the monotheistic Jewish and Christian religions, which it regards as "antecedent revelations," and is heavily influenced by them. The conception of God in these two religions reveals great similarities with that of Islam, as does their view of mankind as God's creation with the freedom to choose between good and evil.

One particular feature common to all three religions is the great significance they attach to the prophets as messengers of God and preachers of the divine revelation. In fact, in Islam, Abraham (Ibrahim) is considered to be the first to profess monotheism and therefore seen as the prototype Muslim; Moses (Musa) is revered as the great law-giver and bringer of the Torah; Jesus (Isa) is the preacher of the Gospel and is regarded as the

The Archangel Israfil sounds the Last Judgment
1370–1380
Iraqi miniature, Washington, Freer Gallery of Art

The Archangel Israfil is as important in Islam as in Judaism and Christianity (where he is known as Raphael). The Last Judgment, announced in all three religions by a trumpet fanfare, is described in the Qur'an, along with the joys of paradise and the torments of hell, in very colorful terms.

St. Peter's in Rome
Photograph taken 1965

The resplendent papal cathedral, completed in the 16th century, is the symbolic center of Catholic Christianity.

direct precursor of Muhammad, who will return at the end of time to rule as a righteous Muslim. However, the emphasis placed on Jesus Christ as the Son of God and as a divine figure is regarded as the distorted exaggeration of the Christians.

With Muhammad, the Revelation of God was brought to its conclusion, hence his epithet "Seal of the Prophets." To the Islamic mind, Muhammad was not founding a new religion but restoring the belief in the One God that had existed since ancient times. On a practical level, Islam adopted many of Judaism's laws regarding food—for example, the prohibition against eating pork or blood and also most of its rules concerning ritual purification. During the (European) Middle Ages in particular, Jews living within the Islamic sphere of influence enjoyed great cultural autonomy and were highly

respected as traders. It was only the Jewish settlement of Palestine that began in the late 19th century and continued during the 1930s and the founding of the state of Israel in 1948 that attracted the enmity of many Muslim countries, but these disputes are not so much the expression of a religious conflict as of a national and territorial one.

The relationship between Islam and Christianity has often proved difficult and full of tension in the past, particularly as a result of the claims of absolute truth made by both these religions, which have frequently resulted in uncompromising militancy. There were repeated periods of peaceful coexistence during the Middle Ages. Today the relationship is characterized not only by intense and enthusiastic activity in the field of cultural exchange, but also by the experiences of the Islamic world under the former Christian colonial powers.

Below:
The holy *Ka'bah* in Mecca

According to Islamic tradition, the cube-shaped meteorite that is the principal Muslim shrine inside the Great Mosque of Mecca was built by Abraham. It is the destination of the annual pilgrimage, the *hajj* and entry is strictly prohibited to non-Muslims. Inside the *Ka'bah* is the Black Stone, believed to have been brought to earth by the Archangel Gabriel.

Above:
The Wailing Wall in Jerusalem, (after 20 CE), the western retaining wall of the temple square

The Wailing Wall is the last surviving wall of the temple, which had been rebuilt by Herod and was destroyed by the Romans in 70 CE. After Jerusalem was conquered by the Arabs it became for the Jews a place of prayer, a meeting place and a place where the destruction of the temple could be mourned. During the Six-Day War (1967), it was annexed by the Jews and is regarded today as a national symbol. The area on which it stands was turned into a holy site.

Meetings of Different Faiths

There shall be no compulsion in religion.

Sura 2

Islam's relationship with other religions has varied greatly from period to period. As Islam can only be embraced of one's own free will and without external compulsion, missionary work does not form part of its teachings. This was also evident in the spread of early Islam: its rapid and triumphant progress led to the establishment of an Arab-Muslim ruling class in the conquered lands, while the subjugated population adhered to its old religion. The People of the Book, the Jews and Christians, who were later joined by the Zoroastrians and, to a certain extent, the Hindus, following the expansion of the Islamic lands, were regarded in areas of Muslim rule as "protected peoples" —meaning they were required to pay a fixed "poll tax" in exchange for which they could continue practicing their religion while enjoying a large measure of cultural autonomy. However, a prerequisite of this tolerance was that they recognized the political sovereignty of Islam and did not contravene its laws.

The Prophets Moses and Muhammad with the Archangel Gabriel
Berlin, Museum of Islamic Art

But the "protected peoples" often possessed only restricted opportunities for social mobility and did not enjoy real equality in the eyes of the law, so many converted to Islam. These "new converts" were to become a significant force, primarily in Spain.
Islam dealt very differently with adherents of natural religions, regarded as polytheists—in particular, the tribal peoples of Africa. For a long time, especially in Sudan, these peoples were enslaved—as they were by the Christians—and beginning with the militant Berber Almoravid and

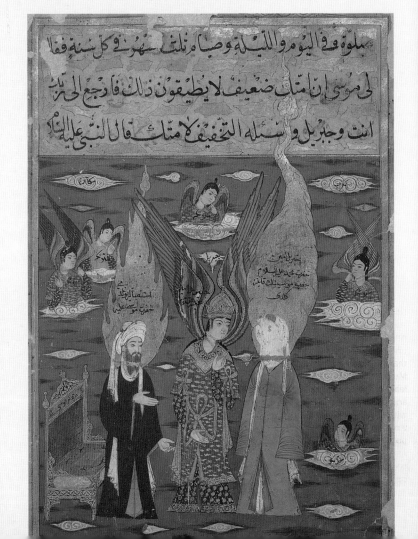

many elements from Islam and saw Muhammad as his direct predecessor as Prophet. This claim was seen by Muslims as an attack on Muhammad as the "Seal of the Prophets," and hence followers of the Bahai faith are subject to severe repression even today, particularly in Iran (their land of origin). The rise of nationalism in Muslim countries at the beginning of the 20th century led to the problem of smoothing over religious differences in favor of common membership of a unified nation, which would have meant granting full legal and social equality to ethnic and religious minorities. In practice, the conservative Muslims and Islamic fundamentalists in some countries try to reject these demands, which are often laid down in law. But in general the official representatives of Islam— for example, those at the head of the al-Azhar University in Cairo, the most important of the Sunni universities—are constantly seeking to intensify the dialogue with other religions, in particular Judaism and Christianity.

Almohad movements (11th–13th centuries) were also at times forcibly converted, as polytheism is regarded as Islam's gravest sin. In Southeast Asia though, Islam arrived by peaceful means, with the Arabic traders who started to arrive in the 13th century, and often formed amazing hybrids by blending with local religions.

One of Islam's original doctrines divided the world into the "dar al-Islam" (house of Islam) in which peace reigned, and the "dar al-Harb" (house of war), which needed to be brought under Islamic rule. Given that even the Prophet Muhammad, as a political leader, concluded treaties and entered into alliances with his opponents, this world view has never been politically implemented. As with nearly all religions, particular problems are caused for Islam by splits

within its own ranks. In addition to the frequently violent struggles between movements that have split off in this way, the Bahai faith represents a particular challenge to Islam. Its forerunner, the Babist movement, whose leader Ali Muhammad adopted the name Bab ("the gateway") and declared himself the resurrected 12th imam of the Shiites, had already been wiped out with much bloodshed in Persia in the middle of the 19th century. The ambition of Baha'Ullah (1817–1892), the founder of the Bahais, was to establish a new world religion that would integrate all those that had preceded it. He borrowed

Allah—the One God

The main aspect of the Islamic message is a radical and uncompromising monotheism, which became more pronounced during its struggle with the ancient Arabian polytheism, and adopted many elements of the Judaic and Christian concept of God. According to the Qur'an, God will forgive any sin, should He so choose, except polytheism. Based on the repeated declaration that God neither has children nor family, the argument against polytheism has also, in part, been raised against the Christian notion of the Holy Trinity. Allah is the Creator and Preserver of the universe, Who has determined everything in advance and Who directs the course of events.

Muezzin on the Shar-i Mardan minaret, Afghanistan

The muezzin, who must be "a man of powerful voice," calls the faithful to ritual prayer from his minaret five times a day. In doing so he holds his hands to his face in a symbolic gesture. A *hadith* tells of the devil, wishing to lead mankind into temptation, fleeing as he hears the words of the call to prayer. Among these is the formula "Allahu akbar" (God is great), as well as the Islamic profession of faith.

Divine flowers, 1709 Miniature

As Islam does not permit God to be represented in pictures, symbols such as these "divine flowers" are occasionally used as a way of depicting His glory. Hidden among the petals of the top left-hand flower are Muhammad's ornamental epithets and in those of the flower on the right, the "beautiful names" of Allah. The buds recall the Prophet's first companions, during whose lifetimes they were promised a place in paradise.

He has ordered the world according to the principles of reason, which mankind is also able to recognize. He is a fair and generous God who shows mercy to those who believe in Him and serve Him. However, He also presides over the Last Judgment and judges mankind's deeds—which are recorded in a book by the angels—after death. The Last Judgment is represented as the "Great Catastrophe," which no man can escape. God separates the just from the unjust and rewards the first of these with entry into paradise, while the second are condemned to hell. The delights of paradise and the torments of hell are both vividly described in the Qur'an. Lack of faith is seen as ingratitude in the face of the favors God bestows upon man during his life, and intercession by the angels or prophets is only possible with God's permission and consent.

As in the Judaic and Christian traditions, God made His original covenant with man through Adam, and used the prophets to present His revelations to mankind. As God's creation, however, man is essentially good. The concept of original sin, which is at the heart of Christianity, is alien to Islam, and this leads to a fundamentally positive view of all the different spheres of human life, including sexuality. Man has been given the choice of leading a life pleasing to God and thus to receive salvation. God has given man free will and is therefore responsible for his own actions, and he will be judged on these. Often, however, he is timorous and fickle and therefore in need of God's guidance. Man should remember God through prayer and be constantly aware of the responsibility that has been placed upon him. Islam, like Judaism, conceives of God's transcendence in such a radical way that man can know nothing about the nature of God, other than He is indivisible and unique. But he can rely on God revealing Himself through His laws and the message of the prophets.

Midday prayer in the mosque of Yafros, Yemen

Ritual prayer is one of the fundamental obligations of Islam and is considered particularly commendable when performed in the mosque. As a sign of submission to the will of God, the forehead is touched to the floor during prayer. Islam also embraces the concept of personal prayer, in which the believer turns to God with his specific concerns.

The Five Pillars of Islam

The religious life of Muslims is based on the so-called Five Pillars of Islam, which represent the obligations and responsibilities of all Muslims towards God and their fellow men, and whose purpose is to ensure the cohesion of the Islamic community.

The first pillar is the profession of faith, or *Shahada* ("confirmation, assurance"), whose text is: "I affirm that there is no god other than the One God" (literally, that there is no god other than God) "and I affirm that Muhammad is the Messenger of God." This formula repeats the words spoken to the Prophet by the Archangel Gabriel. Whoever recites them of his own free will three times before witnesses, following sincere self-examination, is received into the community of Muslims—a step that Muslims believe to be irreversible.

The second pillar is that of communal prayer, or *Salat* ("intercession, blessing"). Unlike personal prayer, the *Salat* is performed five times a day at set times and the community is summoned for it by the muezzin, who calls them from the tower of the mosque, the minaret. Prior to *Salat*, believers must perform a series of ritual ablutions, called *wudu*, in order to approach God in a state of external as well as internal purity. Muslims

The Islamic profession of faith (*Shahada*)

The profession of faith emphasizes the indivisibility and uniqueness of God and attests that Muhammad is His messenger. There is both an individual and a communal profession, that accompanies the Muslim throughout his entire life. A popular motif of Islamic calligraphy, it is also whispered into the ears of new-born infants. Membership of the Muslim community is granted to those who recite the *Shahada* consciously and of their own free will before witnesses.

Muslims at Friday prayers in the Great Mosque of Balkh, Afghanistan

The most important prayers are the Friday prayers, but Friday is not a religious day in the usual sense. Men and women kneel down in rows, separated by gender, and present their neighbors with the Friday greeting at the close of ceremonies. The prayers of the faithful in the mosque are led by a prayer leader (imam).

Another of the Muslim's religious duties is payment of the alms tax. Giving voluntary donations over and above this to those in need is regarded as highly commendable. In the Islamic world the beggar is also respected—for reminding his wealthier fellow Muslim of his duty to share and give.

During the fasting month of Ramadan, Muslims refrain from eating and drinking during the day, and reconcile their differences with their enemies. More time is also spent at prayer in the mosque. The end of the fasting period is celebrated in most Islamic countries with a great "Feast of the End of the Fast", which involves processions, banquets and dancing.

the indebted. To this extent it can be seen as the forerunner of the modern-day welfare state.

The fourth pillar is ritual fasting, *Saum*, observed during the month of Ramadan (the ninth month). During this time the believer abstains from eating, drinking and partaking of tobacco between sunrise and sunset. However, fasting should only be undertaken by those whose health is not expected to suffer as a result, and certain groups (such as the sick, pregnant women, or those who do heavy work) are therefore exempted. This physical self-discipline serves the cause of internal purification and penitence.

The fifth pillar is the pilgrimage to Mecca, *Hajj*, which each adult Muslim is expected to make at least once during his lifetime.

can perform their prayers wherever they happen to be at the time, but some of the community must always pray in the mosque. The faithful bow down several times from a standing position, then touch the floor twice with their forehead, while kneeling as a sign of their submission to the will of God. The most important *Salat* is the midday prayer on Fridays.

The third pillar is the alms tax, the *Zakat* (from *zaka*, meaning "to be pure and just"). Originally a voluntary donation, this developed into a tax prescribed by law and levied on profits, cattle, the fruits of the field, merchandise and gold. It is based on the duty of all Muslims, as stressed by Muhammad, to care for their brothers in faith who might be poor or in need, and is primarily used to help widows, orphans, the sick and

The Pilgrimage to Mecca

The fifth pillar of Islam is the pilgrimage (*Hajj*), which all adult Muslims are required to undertake at least once during their lives, providing they are in a position to do so. The pilgrimage takes them to the holy places of Islam in Mecca and its surroundings, and most pilgrims combine this with a visit to Muhammad's house, which today is the Great Mosque of Medina. The model for the *Hajj* is the journey to Mecca that Muhammad undertook during the last year of his life, but many of its elements date back to pre-Islamic times.

The focal point of the pilgrimage is the visit to the *Ka'bah*, the Muslim world's principal shrine, a stone cube draped in black in the inner courtyard of the Great Mosque in Mecca, which houses the sacred Black Stone. Tradition has it that the meteorite was placed in this building by Abraham. The great pilgrimage, which attracts hundreds of thousands of Muslim pilgrims from all over the world, takes place every year between the 8th and the 12th of the month of pilgrimage.

Before commencing the pilgrimage, the faithful must make sure they are in a state

Pilgrims wearing *ihram* garments about to arrive in Saudi Arabia

of consecration (*ihram*), which they display to the outside world by donning simple white garments. During the pilgrimage they refrain from cutting their hair, shaving, wearing perfume, hunting and sexual intercourse.

Once in Mecca, pilgrims firstly circle the *Ka'bah* seven times before wandering, again seven times, between the hills of al-Safa and al-Marwa, which have now been leveled, as a way of remembering the hardships endured by Abraham's concubine, Hagar, and her son, Ishmail, during their time wandering the desert. In order to save them, God brought forth the spring of Zamzam from the sand of the desert. This water is

White-clad Muslims on the pilgrimage to Mecca
1676
Indian miniature

believed to work miracles and is still drunk by the faithful today.

On the ninth of the month the pilgrims make the journey together to Mount Arafat, which is 15 miles (25 kilometers) away, where they pray and meditate in a standing position from noon until sunset. After sunset they embark on the journey to Mina, which is broken with an overnight stop in Muzdalifa. In Mina, the pilgrims gather seven small pebbles which, on the morning of the 10th, are cast onto column-like stone piles. This custom is supposed to recall

Opposite:
The *Ka'bah* in Mecca,
Saudi Arabia

Abraham, who remained steadfast in his faith and resisted temptation even when God commanded him to sacrifice his son. The three-day "Feast of the Sacrifice" is then held in memory of this trial. From the 12th of the month onwards the pilgrims return to Mecca in order to complete seven farewell circuits of the *Ka'bah*. The importance of the pilgrimage is also revealed by the legal framework surrounding it. Anyone who is unable (for proper reasons) to make the pilgrimage in person can nominate and equip a "deputy" to go instead. Family members can even send a deputy to Mecca on behalf of deceased relatives who were unable to make the pilgrimage.

Festivals and Holidays

The Islamic calendar contains two canonical feasts, each of which are celebrated for three days and nights. The first is the "Feast of the End of the Fast" (Eid al-Fitr), which brings the month of Ramadan to an end. It is lavishly and joyfully celebrated, providing a stark contrast with the muted life led during the fasting month itself. The second, the "Feast of the Sacrifice" (Eid al-Adha), represents one of the high points of the pilgrimage to Mecca and is celebrated by Muslims throughout the world, with the slaughtering of sheep, most of whose meat is distributed to the poor and to friends.

Other festivals and holidays are closely connected to the life of the Prophet: the first day of Muharram, the Islamic New Year's Day, is a

Military games on horseback at the end of the fasting month of Ramadan, Morocco

day for remembering the *Hijrah*, Muhammad's emigration to Medina. A major celebration is held on the 12th day of Rabi al-awwal (the third month) for Muhammad's birthday. The "Night of Determination" on the 27th of Ramadan, during which the revelation of the Qur'an was first

Many Islamic religious festivals have a strong regional character or adopt the rituals of particular tribal cultures. An example of this is provided by the Berber tribes found primarily in the southern regions of the Maghreb countries and who often still lead a nomadic existence. They are the original inhabitants of the Maghreb, who in the 8th and 9th centuries came to be dominated by a city-oriented Arab ruling class. Even today they rarely belong to the ruling elite of their native countries, but nevertheless try to maintain their own culture and language. Around 40 percent of the population in Morocco, a third in Algeria, and a quarter in Libya, speak in Berber tongue. Riding games are popular with the Berbers. Competitors not only display their expert horsemanship, but also demonstrate their prowess with weaponry by shooting at targets with their long rifles while at full gallop.

Celebration of Muhammad's birthday in Akbar Nagar, Bihar

The feast of the Prophet's birthday is the high point of all the celebrations connected with the life of Muhammad. As a sign of adoration, believers process wearing the white pilgrim's tunic and carrying flags and banners in the green of the Prophet, who is believed to have lain on a blanket of green silk after he was born.

Islamic "Feast of the Sacrifice" in an Alevitic village, Turkey

The "Feast of the Sacrifice"—the most important of the Islamic festivals—is celebrated by Muslims during the pilgrimage to Mecca with the slaughtering of a sheep. This is done in memory of Abraham, who was prepared to sacrifice his son when commanded to do so by God, and to commemorate the saving of the son through God's mercy. Most of the animal is given to the poor.

made to Muhammad, is reserved as a day for religious contemplation.

Many festivals, above all in the Maghreb and in Southeast Asia, are specific to certain regions, and dedicated to local saints and their places of burial. The Islamic orthodoxy tolerates such festivals, without officially encouraging them.

The Shiites also observe feast days associated with the lives of the imams. These are mostly celebrated with pilgrimages to their tombs. The 10th day of Muharram (the first month), the martyrdom of the grandson of the Prophet and third imam Hussein, at Kerbela in 680 CE, is particularly remembered. Processions turn to be displays of collective mourning in the form of self-flagellation and passion plays.

Festival being celebrated in open landscape
1599/1600
Turkish miniature
Dresden, State Library of Saxony

In addition to the religious festivals, other large festivals were once celebrated by Islamic rulers and merchants in palaces or in the open air. The rules of hospitality still state that, on certain occasions, the prosperous should entertain their guests with food and artistic performances. As many people as possible are invited to a celebration of this kind.

The Mosque

The word "mosque" means a "place of prostration before God." There are no instructions in either the Qur'an or the *hadiths* for how these mosques should be built, but right from the outset, Muhammad's house in Medina was taken as the obligatory model. The prayer space itself, consisting of a courtyard surrounded by walls, created a spatial separation from their surroundings for the mosques that came afterwards, and the shade-giving roofs made of palm leaves that lined these walls served as a model for the early columned hall mosques. In contrast to Christian churches, mosques do not contain any sculptures or altars, and no liturgical rites such as Communion are

Above:
Exterior of the Blue Mosque in Istanbul 1609–1616

This mosque, built by Sultan Ahmed I, takes its name from its blue interior paintwork. The central dome bordered by half-domes is typical of the Ottoman empire.

Left:
View of the prayer hall of the Great Mosque of Damascus, Syria 706–714/15 CE

This triple-aisled building was the main mosque of the Umayyad caliphs. With its high columns and generous arches above, this mosque is strongly reminiscent of the construction of many Christian churches. There are large mosaics depicting cityscapes and plants on the exterior walls of the inner courtyard. These elements illustrate that the unique characteristics of Islamic art were yet to develop, although the large, spacious prayer hall is already a feature here.

performed in them. The mosque is not only a place of prayer but also a place where communal gatherings can be held, and business transactions conducted. Travelers and those without means can use the mosque as a place of rest, and the persecuted as a place of asylum. As a result of these religious and social functions, the relevant complexes of buildings soon came to be built on to them—such as universities, hospitals, kitchens for the poor, and living accommodation for ascetics and mosque personnel. Additionally, they often served as the burial places of saints.

A distinction is generally made between the simple everyday mosques and the large, central Friday mosques in the cities, in which the Friday sermons are delivered. There are certain elements that are common to all Islamic mosques: the wall to which the faithful turn in order to pray is always oriented towards Mecca. This *qibla* wall contains a prayer niche (*mihrab*), often richly decorated and flanked by two pillars, in which the community's prayer leader (*imam*) kneels. Next to it is the movable pulpit (*minbar*), traditionally made of wood. Steps lead up to a platform on which the preacher stands to deliver the midday sermon on Friday. Most mosques are very sparingly furnished, but numerous imposing chandeliers or mosque lamps are often used to light the room.

In the courtyard of the mosque there is usually a fountain used for the ritual ablutions that precede prayer. Another traditional feature of the exterior is the high tower (*minaret*) from which the caller to prayer (*muezzin*) summons the faithful. Over the course of time the single

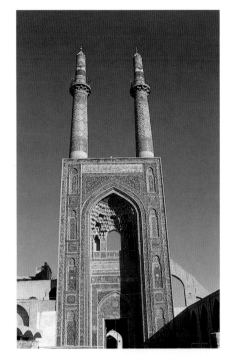

Portal and minarets of the Great Mosque of Yazd,
Iran, from 1325

This portal, a classic *iwan* portal from the time of the Ilkhanids, is surmounted by two slender minarets with circular balconies, and the whole ensemble is decorated with faïence tiles.

Below:
Prayer niche in the main *iwan* of the Sultan Hasan Mosque in Cairo
1356–1363

The precious materials used in the decoration of this Mamluk *mihrab* flanked by columns are shown off here to their best advantage. Immediately next to the prayer niche stands the *minbar*.

high minaret has often been replaced by two or four smaller ones taking the form of corner pillars, which border the building symmetrically.

Various mosque types, such as the columned hall mosque and the *iwan* mosque, can be traced back to pre-Islamic models. The *iwan* is an open, barrel-vaulted gate hall taking the form of a single entrance portal (as in Samarqand) or used in a cruciform, four-*iwan* arrangement with the halls positioned opposite each other (as in Isfahan). The mosques built during the Ottoman empire have a similar character in their mighty central-dome construction surrounded by two, three or four very slender minarets and numerous smaller domes, as seen in the Blue Mosque in Istanbul.

The Spread of Islam

The triumphal march of Islam began immediately after the death of Muhammad with the founding of an empire that, by the start of the eighth century, stretched from Spain in the west to India in the east. The time of the Four Rightly Guided Caliphs (632–661 CE) is considered to have been a period of rule by pious and fair men who had been closely associated with Muhammad. But it was under their rule that the split between the Sunnis and Shiites occurred. This split has lasted to the present day. The cause was that the fourth caliph, Ali, was viewed by a minority, the Shiites, as the sole legitimate successor to the Prophet. Ali and his successors formed the beginning of a sequence of Shiite imams.

Under the hereditary caliph dynasties that followed the assassination of the fourth Caliph, Ali, there occurred a division into different spheres of culture that were initially of an Arabic and Persian character (661–1258). In the early 19th century the Islamic world began to be colonized by the European colonial powers. This, in turn, led to the rise of the liberation movements that resulted in Islamic countries regaining their independence in the 20th century.

Mosque in Mali

During every age, God in His wisdom chooses one man from among men, bestows upon him finery and the distinction of ruler, places in his hands the good of the world and the peace of God's servants and through him closes the gate on corruption, confusion and rebellion. God fills men's eyes with the radiance of His Chosen One, and their hearts with reverence for him, so that they may live their lives in the knowledge of his justice, enjoy the security he confers and plead for the continuance of his reign.

The ruler selects his officials and their aides from among his people and gives each of them a position and a rank. He relies on them to perform the important sacred and profane tasks. His subjects will then trust the path of obedience and go about their work, and the ruler will shelter them from agitation so that under the shade of his justice they may spend their days in peace.

Nizam al-Mulk (1018–1092), Seljuk grand vizier, in his *Book of Statecraft*

Opposite:
Muhammad at the Battle of Badr, 1700
Turkish miniature

Imam Ali and his sons
Qajar miniature

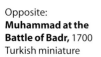

The Four Rightly Guided Caliphs

At the time of his death in 632 CE, the Prophet had left no instructions concerning his succession. Therefore the tribes elected his closest associates as caliphs (from the Arabic *khalifa*, meaning "deputy" or "successor"). These caliphs were at first regarded simply as representatives with respect to their function as leader of the community, but they soon emphasized their dual claim to religious and political leadership through the adoption of the title "Prince of the Faithful." The time of the Four Rightly Guided Caliphs—the first two were fathers-in-law of Muhammad, the last two

Muhammad and the Four Rightly Guided Caliphs
16th century
Ottoman miniature
Cairo, National Library

The period of rule of the Four Rightly Guided Caliphs is regarded by Sunni Muslims as a time of strict adherence to the laws of God, and is still used as a model in discussions about a just social system today, even though the religious and political unity of the Muslims was to collapse under the third and fourth caliphs.

Abu Bakr, the first of the Four Rightly Guided Caliphs
16th century
miniature
Istanbul, Topkapi Palace Library

Muhammad's father-in-law is regarded by Sunni Muslims as the greatest of Muslims outside the Prophet's immediate family. He led community prayers during Muhammad's illness, and was considered the worthiest individual to succeed him. He was able to assert his authority and prevent the outbreak of tribal rivalries by using the slogan "Muhammad is dead, but Allah lives!"

were sons-in-law—is regarded by the majority of Muslims as a golden age during which the community lived strictly by the laws of God.

Abu Bakr (632–634 CE), the Prophet's closest friend, forced the quarreling tribes to unite under his authority and brought Yemen under the control of the new religion.

His successor Umar (634–644 CE), a skillful politician and the most forceful personality among the early caliphs, conquered Syria, Palestine, Egypt, Iraq and Persia during his successful early campaigns. He also gave the new world religion, which was spreading rapidly, its first fixed state structures. Thus he introduced a poll tax for non-Muslims living in occupied areas and, with the establishment of military garrisons, laid the foundations for the conquest of the whole of North Africa from the middle of the 7th century onwards.

The pious and unworldly Uthman (644–656 CE) gave the Qur'an the form it retains today, but state authority continually eluded him.

Finally Ali (656–661 CE), the last of the Rightly Guided Caliphs, was a brave religious debater, a just ruler and a talented didactic poet. He did, however, have many opponents and was politically hesitant, which resulted in him quickly losing political control. Muawiya, the governor of Syria, disputed his right to the caliphate and, in order to prevent a battle taking place, Ali let a court of arbitration settle the question of who the lawful ruler should be.

Islam's first religious schisms took place under Ali: in 657 CE the highly strict Kharijites ("seceders"), who viewed Ali's submission to the court of arbitration as a betrayal of his authority, split away and later formed their own state. The split to have the most far-reaching consequences was between the majority of Muslims (the Sunnis) and Ali's own supporters (the Shiites).

With the exception of Abu Bakr, the first, all the early caliphs were assassinated.

Muslims and Christians in the battle for Jerusalem
13th century

Jerusalem is a holy city for Jews, Christians and Muslims alike, and has been a source of conflict right up to the present day. Under the tolerant control of the Muslims from 638 CE, the "liberation" of Jerusalem was the stated aim of the Christian crusades of the 11th century. After their conquest of the city in 1099, the crusaders instigated a horrific massacre of Muslims, Jews and oriental Christians. When Saladin retook the city for Islam in 1187, he conducted himself chivalrously, forbidding his troops from attacking any section of the population. He released the European Christians against payment of a ransom. He also reopened Jerusalem to people of all faiths.

Sunnis and Shiites

The Shiites, or Shia, are a Muslim minority group that split away from the majority of Muslims or Sunnis (from *sunna*, meaning "custom") and now make up around 10 to 12 percent of all Muslims. They are particularly strongly represented in certain regions—notably Iran and the south of Iraq—and have exerted a significant influence on the history and intellectual life of Islam. The split dates back to the period immediately following the death of Muhammad. Its cause was the question of who should be appointed leader of the young community. A significant role was played from the outset by Ali (602–661 CE), the Prophet's cousin and

The Shiite al-Kazimain Mosque in Baghdad

son-in-law, who had married Muhammad's youngest daughter, Fatima. His supporters saw him as the sole legitimate successor and formed themselves into a group known as the party of Ali ("Shiat Ali"), from which their name is taken. At the heart of their belief are a few words of Muhammad's in praise of Ali, found in the Qur'an. However, the meaning of these is not entirely clear. For the Sunnis, Ali is simply the last of the Four Rightly Guided Caliphs, while for the Shiites he was Muhammad's only legitimate successor. After Ali's assassination they refused to recognize the caliphal dynasty of the Umayyads, which was just beginning to assert itself, or later that of the Abbasids. Instead they revered their

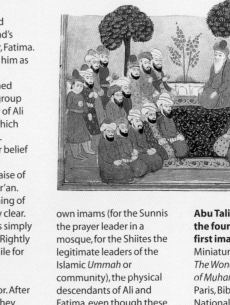

own imams (for the Sunnis the prayer leader in a mosque, for the Shiites the legitimate leaders of the Islamic *Ummah* or community), the physical descendants of Ali and Fatima, even though these were excluded from any real power. For the Shiites, the caliphate represented the illegitimate "rule of kings." Their conception of the imam is of a charismatic spiritual leader, able to pride himself on his descent from the family of the Prophet, who sets a virtuous example for others to follow. This imam-based faith soon took on the characteristics of belief in a savior and became associated with the return of the "awaited one", or Mahdi (*al-mahdi*, literally "the rightly guided one"). This would only happen were the existing order to be overthrown, and so Shiite groups were often the driving force behind

Abu Talib, father of Ali, the fourth caliph and first imam
Miniature from
The Wonderful Story of Muhammad
Paris, Bibliothèque Nationale

socio-revolutionary movements and political Utopias, and characterized by an impatient yearning for salvation. At the same time, the Shiites developed sophisticated cosmologies and adopted intellectual ideas from the Persian cultural region in particular, thereby exercising a constant appeal to intellectuals. In terms of the practical aspects of its religious obligations, the Shiism displays great similarities with Sunnism, although there are also a few characteristic differences—for example, the additional financial contributions required of Shiites, which are held in

trust for the return of the imam at the end of time. The specific event that led to the founding of the Shiite movement was the fate of the third imam, Hussein, son of Ali and Fatima. He became leader of the Shiites after the abdication of his older brother Hassan (the second imam), and was abandoned by his allies during a half-hearted attempted uprising, and surrounded and massacred, along with his entire family group—a total of 72 people—by the troops of the Umayyad caliph Yazid in October 680 CE. This event gave rise to a Shiite cult devoted to the martyr and is re-enacted annually, especially in Iran and Iraq, in plays accompanied by mourning processions and self-flagellation. Leaving aside the extremist groups, three different strands, named after the number of imams they recognize, can be identified within the Shia:

a) For the Fiver Shiites, or Zaydis, the line of legitimate imams ends with Zayd, a son of the fourth imam, who was killed during a rebellion against the Umayyads around 740 CE. The Fivers reject the principle of inheritance when choosing their imam, in favor of supporting the claim of the most suitable candidate. They are regarded as tolerant and are the closest of the Shiite groups to the Sunnis. They do not share the Shiite belief in the return of the lost imam. The smallest group within the Shia, the Zaydis ruled Yemen for over 1000 years, from 901 to 1962.

b) The Sevener Shiites, or Ismailis, take their name from Ismail, a son of the sixth imam, who died in 760 CE. They are the least united and most secretive of the Shiite lines, and are distinctive for their philosophical speculation and socio-revolutionary outlook as well as their belief in the lost imam. They attained a special significance with the Egyptian caliphate of the Fatimids (909–1171). The feared Assassins (from the Arabic *hashishiyun*, meaning "hashish eaters"), who murdered kings and caliphs in spectacular fashion and thus gave their name to the term used in many Romance languages, were also Ismailis. The Ismailis eventually split into two groups and today live for the most part in India. The head of the line known as the "Hodjas" is the Aga Khan.

c) The Twelver Shiites, or Imamis, are the largest group of Shiites, and recognize a sequence of 12 imams, the last of whom, Muhammad al-Mahdi, went "into hiding" as a child in 873/874 CE in order to escape from the caliphs. Twelvers believe that he will return at the end of time as the Mahdi. The Twelver Shiites acquired special importance when the Safavids made their branch of the Shia the official religion of Iran in 1501.

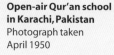

Open-air Qur'an school in Karachi, Pakistan
Photograph taken
April 1950

There the rank of mullah (from the Arabic *maula*, meaning "lord") was to develop as a form of Shiite clergy, which, since the 19th century, has increasingly opposed the secularization of the state and was one of the driving forces behind the revolution in 1978/79. Ayatollah ("sign of God," the title given to senior mullahs) Khomeini used the Shiite yearning for salvation and revolutionary fervor to proclaim his theocratic "Islamic Republic of Iran."

Shiite flagellants on the streets of Rawalpindi, Pakistan, marking the anniversary of Hussein's death

The Early Empires

The first caliph dynasty, that of the Umayyads (661–750 CE), was founded by Muawiya, the governor of Syria, who had successfully rebelled against Caliph Ali. He abandoned the principle of tribal election and made the caliphate hereditary within his family. The largely Arab Umayyads, whose traditional seat was Damascus, provided the empire with efficient administrative structures, constructed Islam's first major public building, and repeatedly attacked the Byzantine empire. During a second wave of conquests, their armies occupied North Africa and Spain to the west, as well as parts of Pakistan to the east, and from these positions pushed out towards France and Central Asia. However, the Umayyads constantly

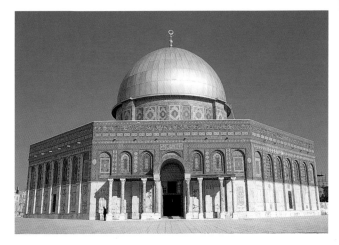

had to tackle the problem of religious unrest within their empire, which finally led to them being overthrown by the Abbasids.

The Abbasid caliph dynasty (750–1258) moved its seat to the newly established city of Baghdad, and began to bolster the caliph empire

The Dome of the Rock in Jerusalem
691/692 CE

An Umayyad structure houses the rock from which, traditionally, Muhammad departed on his night journey to heaven.

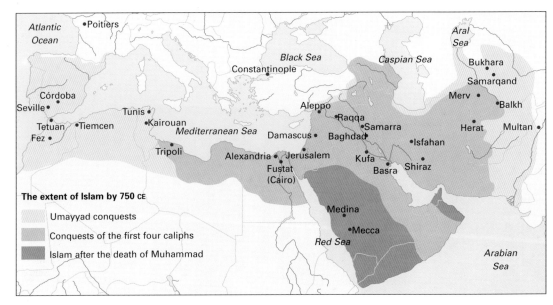

The extent of Islam by 750 CE

- Umayyad conquests
- Conquests of the first four caliphs
- Islam after the death of Muhammad

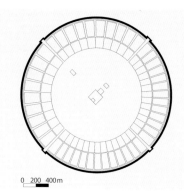

The round city of Baghdad (from 762 CE)
Reconstruction

In 762 CE the second Abbasid caliph, al-Mansur (754–775 CE), founded Baghdad as a Utopian circular city at the center of which stood the great mosque and the palace of the caliph. Its transparent layout was supposed to bring about improved hygiene and facilitate social control.

Below:
View of Fez, Morocco

The city of Fez, founded in 807 CE, was enlarged by the Almohads in the 12th century to become the center of western Islam. By the 13th century it already had a population of over 200,000, and the city remains an important religious and cultural center today.

The Great Mosque of al-Mutawakkil in Samarra, Iraq
848–852 CE

After the Abbasids moved their seat to Samarra in 836 CE, Caliph al-Mutawakkil (847–861 CE) constructed what at the time was Islam's largest mosque, able to accommodate over 180,000 of the faithful. Its colossal spiral minaret, the Malwiya—the design of which goes back to that of the old Babylonian temple towers, known from the story of the Tower of Babel—was to become the mosque's emblem. Other imposing palaces and mosques were built, although the caliphs finally moved back to Baghdad in 892 CE, which meant Samarra lost its important role.

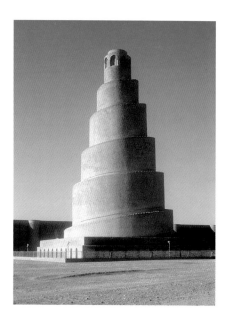

internally through legal reforms and the strengthening of Islamic culture. Under its rule Islam adopted a distinctly Persian character.

Baghdad developed into the world Islamic center for trade, culture, science and philosophy under Caliph Harun al-Rashid (786–809 CE), well known from the *Thousand and One Nights*, and his erudite son al-Mamun (813–833 CE) in particular. But as early as 800 CE the Abbasids had to accept the *de facto* autonomy of certain regions with their own ruling dynasties. Following a period of political decline, the Abbasids fell under the protection of different, mostly Turkish, military dynasties from the middle of the 10th century onwards, and had not yet been able to liberate themselves from these when they were overthrown by the Mongols in 1258.

Arabs and Persians

Following the Arab and Persian-dominated early period of Islam's history, power started to shift to other peoples as the religion spread. Even during Abbasid rule, the Arab-controlled territory had begun to degenerate and break up politically into a sequence of autonomous local and regional princedoms. The most important of these was the emirate of the Spanish Umayyads of Córdoba (756–1031), who ruled Spain and parts of North Africa, making Córdoba the cultural center of Islam's western region. In 929 CE the Umayyads adopted the title of caliph. A significant competitor to Baghdad and Córdoba developed in the form of the Shiite countercaliphate of the Fatimids (909–1171) in Tunisia and Egypt, who built Cairo into one of the major cultural centers of the Muslim world. For a while they also had sovereignty over the holy places of Mecca and Medina, although the general situation in central Arabia continued to be char-

Alhambra, view of the Court of the Lions in Granada
14th century

The Alhambra was the center of government of the Nasrids, the last Muslim dynasty in western Europe (1232–1492). Although their political significance as vassals of the more powerful Christian kings of Spain was relatively small, their rulers distinguished themselves as sophisticated patrons of architecture. The Court of the Lions, built in the 14th century and enclosed by arcades, possesses a central fountain whose water basin rests on stone, water-spouting lions. The magical beauty of this building made the Alhambra the focal point of a yearning for all aspects of the Orient in the 19th century.

acterized by the region's numerous independent tribes and clans.

During the time of the crusades, from the end of the 11th century onwards, real power in the Islamic world lay with military dynasties such as the Ayyubids in Egypt and Syria (1171–ca. 1260). Their founder, Saladin retook Jerusalem from the crusaders in 1187 and earned much

Floor tiles depicting the battle between King Richard I and Saladin
Around 1290
Chertsey Abbey, Surrey, Great Britain

Sultan Saladin (1138–1193) and Richard Coeur de Lion, king of England (1157–1199) were the leaders of the Muslims and Christians respectively at the time of the crusades. They were very evenly matched, and when a cease-fire was agreed in 1192, they even discussed a possible marriage between Saladin's brother and Richard's sister, who would have ruled over Jerusalem in the name of both religions.

mysticism ever since the time of the Abbasids, experienced a long period of foreign rule by Arabs, Turks and Mongols. Only with the arrival of the Safavid dynasty (1501–1722) did the "special development" of Persia within Islam begin. The Safavids elevated the Twelver branch of the Shia to the state religion and led the empire culturally into a golden age, whose influence has endured into present-day Iran. Through his policy of equality between the different groups and the settling of Caucasian peoples in Persia, Shah Abbas the Great (1587–1629), who made Isfahan the empire's new capital, also laid the foundations for a nation state whose structures were maintained by succeeding dynasties.

praise, both in the Orient and in the Occident, for his chivalry. The dynasty that followed—that of the Mamluks (1250–1517), who had originally been military slaves—drove the last of the crusaders out of Palestine, and in 1260 held up the Mongol's march westward.

Since the 11th century, northern Africa and Spain had been ruled by aggressive and puritanical Berber dynasties, but gradually Spain was lost to the Christians. In the struggle between the Christian and Islamic powers for supremacy in the Mediterranean, northern Africa (with the exception of Morocco) fell under the sovereignty of the Turkish Ottomans, who occupied practically the whole of the Arabian cultural area, in the 16th century.

Persia, which had overshadowed Islamic philosophy, poetry and

Turks and Mongols

The Turks were originally nomads from Central Asia who lived in their own tribal groups. During their migration westward, they often entered the service of Islamic rulers as mercenaries and military leaders, but also, from the 9th century, they began to create their own empires and converted to Islam. The most important Turkish dynasties of the early period were those of the Ghaznavids (977–1186), the Seljuks (1038–1194) and the Khwarazm-Shahs (1097–1231). As the Turks could not lay claim to any kinship with the Prophet Muhammad, they

Sultan Suleyman
Painting
Istanbul, Topkapi
Palace Library

Under Suleyman the Magnificent (1520–1566), the Ottoman empire reached its territorial and cultural peak. Following victories in the Maghreb and the Balkans, he dedicated himself to the development of Istanbul and to the strengthening of the political structure of his empire. For this he was given the title "Law-giver" by the Turks.

The Ottoman army besieging Vlenna in 1529
1588, miniature from the *Hunername*
Istanbul, Topkapi
Palace Library

After the King of Hungary died in battle against the Turks (1526), his country was occupied by the Holy Roman Emperor's armies in the west, and the Ottomans in the east. The great powers of the Christian and Muslim worlds now stood face to face. King Ferdinand annexed central Hungary in 1528, and was repulsed by the Ottomans, who lay siege to Vienna, but ultimately failed to capture the city.

became strictly orthodox protectors of the Islamic Sunna—that is, they recognized the caliph dynasties as the Prophet's successors.

The Seljuks placed the caliphs of Baghdad under their protection and ruled their empire, which stretched from Anatolia to Central Asia (including the Arabian Peninsula and Persia) through a network of Sunni universities (*madrasas*). At the end of the 12th century they were superseded by their former vassals, the Khwarazm-Shahs.

The Mongols, led by Genghis Khan, began their sweeping march west in 1218, overrunning the land and bringing large-scale devastation to every empire from Central Asia to eastern Europe. Genghis's grandson Hülägü conquered Persia and in 1258 unleashed the "Mongol storm" on Baghdad, but before long his

Left:
Timur's memorial in Tashkent,
Uzbekistan

From 1370 onwards, Islam's greatest conqueror created a vast empire stretching from Ankara to Delhi. Samarqand became the center of Islamic culture. Timur led his military campaigns skillfully and harshly. He died during a campaign to China. His empire fell apart soon after, due to power struggles between his heirs.

Mahmud crossing the Ganges
Edinburgh University Library

Mahmud of Ghazna (998–1030), known as "Hammer of the Infidels" for his defense of the orthodox Sunna, conquered Afghanistan and northern India during 17 military campaigns undertaken from 1001. He was regarded as the creator of the vast Ghaznavid empire.

successors adopted Islam and founded the Ilkhanid empire (1258–1335). This soon disintegrated into a number of small empires, which Timur Lenk (1328–1405), the greatest conqueror of Islam, finally united to form a single vast empire from 1370 onwards. His descendant, Babur, founded the Mughal empire (1526–1858) of fairy-tale splendor in India, which developed into the most important Islamic empire in the east, but became politically insignificant after 1707. During the Turks' march west, the Turkish Ottoman dynasty eventually reached Asia Minor, where they established a rapidly expanding empire in Anatolia and the Balkans from 1300 onwards, ultimately taking over the Byzantine empire with their capture of Constantinople in 1453. In the 16th century, the Ottomans also conquered North Africa, the Arabian Peninsula and the Mediterranean region, and periodically ruled over southeastern Europe

Taj Mahal in Agra,
India, 1632–1643

This famous tomb, built of white marble by the Mughal ruler Shah Jahan (1627–1658) for his spouse Mumtaz Mahal, is regarded as the high point of Islamic architecture in India, and is often referred to as the "eighth wonder of the world."

as far west as Hungary. Ottoman culture, which also exerted a strong influence on that of Europe, gave rise to a period of unique artistic richness. However, in the 18th century this Islamic world power began to decline politically—a process the reforms undertaken in the 19th century were not able to prevent.

Colonialism and Liberation Movements

The colonialism pursued by the European powers—predominantly France and Great Britain—during the 19th century, affected nearly all the Islamic countries. As early as the 16th century, the Western European maritime powers were establishing trading companies within various Islamic empires, which in time came to dominate local economic life. In 1830, France occupied Algeria and secured the protectorate of Morocco for itself in 1863, and Tunisia in 1881. Meanwhile Great Britain occupied India in 1857 and Egypt in 1882, and operated *de facto* protectorates in the Sudan, Persia and Afghanistan.

The colonial powers brought European settlers to the occupied countries (particularly in the case of

King Faisal I of Iraq
(1883–1933)

Prince Faisal of Mecca, on whom hopes of Arab independence were pinned, was elected king of Syria, Palestine and Jordan by the Arab National Congress in 1920, but was deposed by the French soon after. In 1921, supported by Britain, he became king of Iraq. His brother Abdullah founded the royal house that still rules Jordan today. The brothers were careful rulers, treating different parties and religions in their countries fairly. Even so, Abdullah was murdered in Jerusalem in 1951 and Faisal's grandson, Faisal II, was assassinated in a bloody *coup* by Iraqi army officers in 1958.

Tomb of the Mahdi, Sudan

During the 1881 uprising led by the "Mahdi" Mohammed Ahmed (1844–1885), fanatical religious warriors drove the British out of Egypt and the Sudan, and conquered Khartoum. In 1899, however, the British destroyed the empire of the Mahdi's successor, Abdullah, killing huge numbers of his followers in the process.

the Maghreb), exploited the local economic resources, carried out ambitious technical projects (such as the construction of the Suez Canal in 1869), and put in place administrative and educational systems based on the European model. Their aim was the Europeanization of the indigenous elite. The colonial attitude was often characterized by an arrogant disdain for the Muslim religion, which they viewed as backward.

Britain and France supported the Arabs in their struggle for independence against the Ottoman empire, favoring in their place the Hashimite family of sharifs, who came from Mecca. After the collapse of the Ottoman empire, the mandates over Syria and Lebanon were secured by France; Palestine, Jordan and Iraq by Great Britain. They were not able to prevent the rise of the al-Saud family

Napoleon arriving in Egypt, 1798
Steel engraving from a painting by J.A.Gross

With Napoleon's arrival in Egypt, the Orient once again featured in Europe's consciousness.

At the beginning of the 20th century, liberation movements developed in most countries, with Islam playing an increasingly important role. It became an important factor in shaping the identity and self-awareness of many countries. The end of the Second World War led primarily in the British-occupied regions to the withdrawal of the colonial powers. In 1947 the Muslim state of Pakistan (whose eastern province later became Bangladesh) was a result of the religio-political division of India, which had recently won its independence. Morocco and Tunisia were only granted their independence in 1956, while Algeria's bloody civil war continued until independence was won in 1962.

from central Arabia, whose leader Ibn Saud conquered practically the whole of the Arabian Peninsula along with its holy sites in 1902, and established the kingdom of Saudi Arabia in 1932.

Mosque in Ududdiah, Malaysia

The individual nature of Islam in Southeast Asia can be seen in its mosque architecture. Here are influences of European colonial style and other religions alongside traditional Islamic elements. Following Malaysia's independence (1957), Islam was retained as the state religion, along with guarantees of proper religious freedom for its religious minorities. Today, Malaysia is one of just a few elected monarchies in the world.

Science and Art

The rise of philosophy and natural sciences in the Islamic world between the 9th and 13th centuries was due in part to the adoption of various classical traditions. Islamic scholars took the knowledge of the ancients, above all that of the Greek philosophers, as a starting point for their own research. Nearly all the philosophers were polymath scholars, active as physicians and scientists. Medicine in particular reached a level that surpassed by far that of medieval Europe.

This was also a golden age for literature and Islamic mysticism, Sufism, with its many different strands, was able to benefit from a period of abundant intellectual freedom to flourish alongside the religious orthodoxy. Many mystics grouped themselves into influential orders organized into tight-knit communities.

A true Islamic art, which dealt with the problem of the religion's prohibition of images in a number of different ways, also began to emerge. This fear of the representative in sacred art resulted on one hand in the development of calligraphy as a form of artistic writing, and on the other in a type of ornament based on intertwining geometric and vegetal motifs.

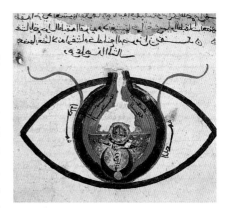

Anatomy of the eye
al-Mutadibi, around 1200
Arabic manuscript
Cairo, National Library

Time in its length is measured out by the lifetimes of successive individuals; the achievements of those who came before are passed onto their descendants so that they accumulate with the heirs, and grow and spread. This is a form of metempsychosis, not the type some believe in, of one soul migrating to the body of another, but rather, the transfer of knowledge from the souls who pass away to the souls who follow after, just as writing is transferred from worn-out pages onto new ones.

Al-Biruni
(973–1048), from
Gardens of Science

Jug from Iran
(probably Kashan)
early 13th century
Underglaze-painted
fritware
Washington, Freer
Gallery of Art

Opposite:
**Mosque of Sheikh
Lutfallah, Isfahan,**
Iran, 1603–1619

The Importance of Philosophy

Islamic philosophy has developed primarily from the high regard in which the Greek classics, particularly the works of Plato and Aristotle (both of whom were seen quite simply as the "teachers"), were held in the Arabian-Persian region. Greek thought was not just studied, but also developed further, along original lines, and combined with the teachings of Islam. A large number of rulers, such as the erudite Caliph al-Mamun, who founded a "house of science" in Baghdad in 833 CE, actively promoted philosophy and other sciences.

The five main spheres of Islamic philosophy were metaphysics, logic, epistemology, ethics, and political philosophy. Under the reign of Abbasid caliphs in the 9th century, a form of rationalism strongly influenced by classical antiquity emerged in the fields of theology and jurisprudence. This was espoused in particular by the Mutazilites, who emphasized man's rationality and freedom in thought and deed. The relationship, often characterized by a spirit of competition, between the more practical, natural science-based Arabian thought and the gnostic-neoplatonic speculation of the Persian tradition, also proved extremely fruitful for the development of Islamic philosophy.

The neoplatonic philosopher al-Kindi (ca. 800–870 CE) synthesized Greek philosophy with the Islamic doctrine of the Prophets and produced some 300 works during his lifetime. The polymath scholar Ibn Sina (980–1037), known in the West as Avicenna, was an outstanding philosopher, natural scientist, and physician. He wrote works on all of these subjects, which, for hundreds of years, were among the most important textbooks in their field. The scholar and physician Ibn Rushd (1126–1198), who was originally from Córdoba and known in the West as Averroes, advocated one of Islamic philosophy's most important aspects—a strongly rational

Socrates debating with his students
13th century
Seljuk manuscript
Istanbul, Topkapi Palace Library

Greek philosophers—in particular Socrates, Plato and Aristotle—occupied such an important position in Arabian–Persian culture that they were revered almost as much as the Prophet, and were regarded as teachers of how man should best use his reason.

conception of God inspired by the ideas of Aristotle. He was attacked by the orthodox scholars for his theory that the world has no beginning and for the thesis that religions are only allegorical masks hiding the one truth, a truth accessible to all men as rational beings. His work was taken up in the West, where it was known as "Latin Averroism." It also influenced the most influential philosopher of the European Middle Ages, Thomas Aquinas, as well as contributing to the popularization of classical philosophy in Europe, which became known primarily through the work of Islamic philosophers.

With the triumphal march of Islamic orthodoxy into all areas of life, classical Islamic philosophy started to decline from the 13th century onwards, although the development of important systems of thought have continued in certain schools right up to the present day.

Statue of Averroes
Córdoba

Islamic philosophy reached its peak with the physician, philosopher and natural scientist, Averroes. He was personal physician to the Almohad caliphs and was entrusted by them with high political office. Thus he was also the senior judge of his native city, Córdoba. The basis of Averroes' thought was the ambiguity of the Qur'an, but he did not consider his ideas to be incompatible with Islam. His rational conception of God influenced the whole medieval debate on the nature of God in both the Christian and the Muslim worlds.

Left:
The bird trap
late 13th century
Illustration from
Kalila and Dimna
Cairo, National Library

A rich tradition of literature developed during the early Islamic period, which included fairy tales as well as philosophical and legal subjects. The collection of fables *Kalila and Dimna* is one of the most important works of classical Islamic literature and describes human behavior using the example of animals and their fate. This collection, originally published in Sanskrit, was repeatedly added to over the course of the centuries and enjoyed such popularity that the manuscripts preserved from the 13th century are among the first Arab manuscripts to be illustrated in miniature. A Spanish translation for King Alfonso the Wise of Castile (1252–1284) was used as the basis for Latin editions, which made the work widely known in the Occident. From the 13th century onwards it became general practice to illustrate important works of Islamic literature.

The Mystics

The Origins of Mysticism

The rich and complex world of Islamic mysticism has always had a difficult relationship with orthodox Islam. It contains many extra-Islamic and pre-Islamic elements, and expresses itself in a curious balance between the ardent rejection of the world and the call for the whole of Islam to undergo a spiritual revival.

As early as the 8th century, mystical tendencies developed within Islam that were based on the Qur'an's praise of asceticism, but whose roots also lay in various forms of worship practiced in the cultures conquered by Islam. The influence of Christian, Hindu and Buddhist monasticism is unmistakable, as are certain philosophical strands from Persia. In addition, particular techniques employed by the mystics, such as trance, rhythmic movement, the recitation of prayer formulas and names, and the invocation of God, are very similar to Indian meditation techniques. From the 10th century onwards, mysticism started to spread throughout the whole of the Islamic world and in certain areas became a veritable mass movement. The early mystics generally wore simple woolen habits, hence the name "Sufi" (from the Arabic *suf*, meaning "wool").

The Search for God

Their early, pious asceticism soon developed into a deliberate search for God, centered on notions of fear of and trust in God. It was characterized by a renunciation of the world and the search for inner peace. Meditation and constant contemplation of God played an important role in this: the mystics placed a higher value on the search for God with oneself than on an external adherence to Islamic rules. Part of their search for the intuitive recognition of the God with the "loving heart", was a longing for physical and spiritual proximity to God—this went as far as embracing the idea of actually merging with the divine.

Whirling dervishes around 1800, French copperplate engraving

Mystic Poetry

Many mystics devoted themselves to the study of music and poetry, particularly Persian didactic poetry, which was sought to develop an individual theory of love. Its language is often characterized by a strong sensuality and natural piety. One particular high point of this mystic poetry is represented by the work of Jalal al-Din

Whirling dervishes in a dervish school in Üsküdar Istanbul

Rumi (1208–1273), whose work is distinguished by its great richness of imagery, and who founded the order of the Whirling Dervishes in Konya, Turkey.

Conflicts with Orthodoxy
Because of their teachings and also their language, conflicts between the mystics and orthodox Islam were inevitable. The authorities viewed their desire for oneness with God as blasphemous and were skeptical of the tendency of many mystics, often revered by the people as saints, to preach reform. This mistrust resulted in numerous waves of widespread persecution and executions. The mystic and theologian al-Ghazzali (1058–1111) attempted to reconcile mysticism with orthodox theology and introduced the idea of the intuitive recognition of God into mainstream Islamic theology. His work *The Niche of Lights* was pioneering in terms of the mystics' speculation on the nature of light, according to which God, as the source of all light, illuminates the whole of creation with His glory. Ibn al-Arabi (1165–1250), Andalusia's most important mystic, claimed to have penetrated through to the very nature of God and experienced union with God as a result of the intensity of his belief, thus supposedly earning himself a position higher than the Prophets. He also taught that all created existence would eventually dissolve into God.

Organizational Systems of the Mystics
Numerous communities of mystic orders developed between the 12th and 14th centuries, forming various brotherhoods and federations, as well as establishing monasteries. They strove to achieve a wide-ranging asceticism and were organized along strictly hierarchical lines. At their head stood the sheikh, or order leader, to whom the brothers owed absolute obedience. One rule stated: "In the hand of your sheikh, be as a corpse in the hands of the corpse washer." Many orders combined a life of prayer with a life of fighting: living as frontier warriors in fortified monasteries thus became

Choir of dervishes, 1870
Painting by Wassili W. Werestschagin

a model for the chivalric orders of the Christian world. This is how the Almoravids (1060–1147) set about the Islamization of North Africa and the Sanussi movement conducted its fight for liberation in Libya during the 19th and 20th centuries. The brotherhoods grew rich and powerful as a result of their religious foundations, particularly in the provincial cities of the Ottoman empire. The order members became known as dervishes, a term that probably derives from the Persian word for beggar.

Mysticism Today
Mystics and Sufis have exerted a strong influence on popular forms of Islam and continue to do so. Especially in North Africa and Southeast Asia, many Sufis are united by the idea of magic, holding seances and faith-healing sessions and producing amulets. Often they are also the driving force behind bizarre local cults such as…. Within the framework of esotericism and "new age" practices, various Sufi ideas and writings have also appeared in western culture.

A dervish's begging bowl
made from an Indian fruit
Teheran, Malek Collection

Medicine, Mathematics and Astronomy

The 9th to 13th centuries are regarded as the golden age of Islamic science. But Muhammad had already ordered his followers to "seek after knowledge even unto China" hundreds of years earlier.

Most of the classical philosophers were not only practicing physicians but also natural scientists who were conducting their own research. Arab mathematicians preserved the knowledge of classical antiquity and concerned themselves with such concrete calculations of everyday life, as inheritance portions. Discoveries such as decimal fractions and trigonometry also date back to this time.

In mathematics, astronomy and physics, Islamic philosophers built on the calculations elaborated by the

Avicenna's Canon Medicinae, 980–1037 Damascus, National Museum

Along with the works of al-Razi (865–925), who was the director of hospitals in Rayy and Baghdad, the Canon of polymath scholar Avicenna was regarded as the most important medical textbook in the Islamic regions as well as in Europe, for a period of 500 years. In addition to a number of observations and theories, the Canon also includes a systematic survey of the medical knowledge of the Greek and Islamic worlds. Avicenna led a peripatetic life full of discovery and adventure, and taught at the courts of various different rulers.

ancient Middle Eastern cultures, in particular those of the Babylonians. They not only investigated the motion of the planets, but also undertook astrological speculations on hierarchies and cycles in world events. Al-Biruni (973–1048) in particular, who taught at the court of the Ghaznavids, established a close relationship between astronomy and philosophy in his work *Gardens of Science*.

Cosmology and science formed a basis for the outstanding achievements of the Islamic world in the field

Jai Sing Observatory in Delhi, 18th century

Many rulers devoted themselves to the study of the stars and the calculation of planetary movements. They constructed large observatories, such as this one in Delhi. The author of the most accurate astronomical charts was Ulugh Beg, one of the grandsons of Timur Lenk (Tamerlane).

Astrolabe
14th century
Yellow copper
Damascus, National
Museum

Astrolabes were used
not only for the
sighting of the
planets, but also to
calculate the
direction of prayer
toward Mecca.

Surgery
15th century
Turkish miniature
Istanbul, Millet Library

Surgeons were only
allowed to practice
once they had
completed a period of
further training on
the skull, which
represented the
summit of medical
expertise. Work in
ophthalmology in
particular was
pioneering: Islamic
physicians were able
to list 130 diseases of
the eye and their
remedies. By the year
1000, they could
detach cataracts from
the lens and remove
by suction.

of optics. Around the turn of the 11th
century, Ibn al-Haitham (965–post
1040), the most important physicist of
the Middle Ages, measured the depth
of the earth's atmosphere and was first
to calculate the refraction of light in
the cosmos by measuring the distances
between stars. Observatories were
built throughout the Islamic world
during his life.

The classical medical canon consisted essentially of the writings of
Hippocrates and Galen. Medicine was
divided into the main disciplines of
healing, therapeutics, and ophthalmology—as early as the year 1000
cataracts could be successfully operated on. Islamic medicine was also
the first to describe blood circulation
and the structure of the human heart.

Hospital treatment, especially in the

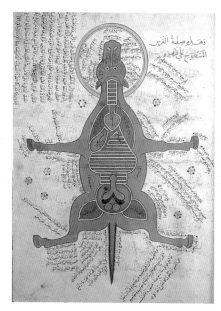

Anatomy of a horse
15th century
Egyptian miniature
Istanbul, University
Library

As there was no
prohibition on
dissection in Islamic
culture, unlike in the

Christian west,
physicians possessed
a good knowledge of
anatomy, and their
textbooks contain
detailed diagrams of
both human and
animal bodies.

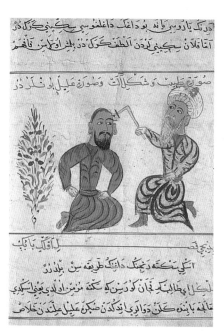

large complexes in Syria and Egypt
and in Baghdad, was exemplary.
There were separate departments for
surgery, orthopedics, treatment of
fever and nutritional problems.
Massage was used as a treatment
and the mentally ill were also cared
for. Additionally, the Islamic medical
encyclopedias were consulted for
the study of medicine in Christian
Europe, which lagged far behind in
terms of medical diagnostics and
standards of hygiene, right up to the
beginning of the modern era.

Image Prohibition

The laws of Islam ordain a fundamental prohibition of images, particularly in the religious sphere, but this has always been subject to a variety of interpretations. The Qur'an makes no clear statement on the subject: Sura 5, 90 names wine, games of chance, divining arrows and idols (graven images) as "abominations devised by Satan," but does not clarify whether this refers to all images or just religious graven images. The *hadiths* are clearer: one declares that on the Day of Judgment, those who make graven images will be punished by God with all the torments of hell until they breathe life into their pictures.

This belief is based on the idea that all depictions of living things expect to be given a soul (brought to life)—which is the task of God, as the sole Creator. The mimicking of life in pictures therefore intrudes upon God's prerogatives, revealing man's presumption in wishing to behave like God. In addition, the idea prevails in popular Islamic belief that the representation of living things is unnatural and gives those responsible for them power over their objects. (This also explains the dislike of many Muslims to be photographed.) From a historical point of view, the sacred has always been treated differently to the profane: while images of living things have always been taboo for the interiors of mosques and *madrasas*, and later for their façades as well, even during Islam's early period the Umayyad caliphs took their cue from the pictorial luxury of late-classical Christianity, and decorated their more important structures and desert palaces with mosaics and cycles of frescos. The stricter application of the prohibition, which came later, favored the development of abstract ornamentation and calligraphy, mainly in the form of large stucco panels or stone inscriptions such as those in the palace city of Medina al-Zahra. As early as 721 CE, Caliph Yazid II issued an edict ordering the destruction of all Christian holy pictures within the

Lion with movable tail
13th century
Bronze
Paris, Louvre

Islamic area, known as iconoclasm, as they represented the worship of graven images. Following the Seljuk's use of major three-dimensional images in the decoration of their façades, miniature painting, which was to use representational images freely, started to emerge as an important aspect of Islamic art from the 14th century onwards. Having started with the illustrations in the *Shahname* and various works of Persian poetry, the first pictorial representations of Muhammad's life began to appear around 1400. However, the Prophet's face was always veiled or depicted as a white space surrounded by a garland of flames. Important schools of painting gradually developed, primarily in the eastern empires of the Timurids, the Ottomans, the Safavids, and the Mughals. In the Safavid empire, the development of painting was further encouraged by the fact that instead of

Muhammad on a trading expedition, second half of the 16th century
Iranian miniature

enforcing the strict prohibition of images, the Shiites regarded the figurative depiction of religious subject matter—the life of Ali, for example—as quite legitimate. This new attitude is also evident in portraiture, with many Ottoman sultans commissioning portraits of themselves from European painters. Puritanical iconoclastic movements such as the Wahabis were to emerge repeatedly, however, with the aim of cleansing the world of graven images: this also included the destruction of the tombs of saints.

Wall panel from the great hall, Medina al-Zahra
936–1010

Calligraphy and Ornament

Islam is described as a book- and writing-dominated culture, due to the fact that the Qur'an is considered to be both the sole direct testimony of God's revelation and the verbatim message of God itself. Its physical form is therefore a reflection of the beauty of the Divine Word and, thus of the beauty of God.

Those who practiced calligraphy, the art of beautiful handwriting, which begun as early as 700 CE, were conscious of the aesthetic aspects of the religion and pursued their craft with great respect. For this reason becoming a calligrapher involved a long and thorough training.

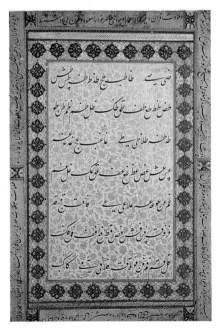

Ornamental page featuring a pious *naskhi* text in the form of a bird (Iran)
17th century
Berlin, Museum of Islamic Art

A not uncommon feature of the art of calligraphy was for religious texts to be given figurative contours taking, for example, the form of birds, ships or even faces. To the strict orthodox authorities monitoring offenses against the prohibition of images, the artist could object that his work was composed of holy names and religious sayings.

Persian calligraphy
Istanbul, Topkapi Palace Library

Persian ornamental pages, whose texts were mainly written in the *nastaliq* script, which originated in Tabriz and spread throughout the whole of Persia, are usually bordered by floral motifs. These texts, written in a light hand, are gems of the Persian poetic arts. As a rule they took the form of individual sheets that were collected in albums or framed and hung on the wall.

The first type of script to develop was the angular and monumental, clear-contoured *Kufic*, based on the ancient writing of the Nabataeans, which remained the main style used for the Qur'an up to the 12th century. Following the introduction of paper into the Islamic world, Arabic script became increasingly geometrical and refined. It was largely influenced by the official style practiced by the Persians and Turks—*flowering Kufic*, distinctive for its meandering, intertwined letters—which was emerging at the time. This tendency was developed further by later decorative styles, which emphasize the ornamental. The peak of this development came with the Persian-Indian *nastaliq*, a form of cursive writing that was usually framed by colorful decorative borders, and the official *divani* script used in official Ottoman documents as well as for the splendidly formed extended signatures of the Ottoman rulers, the sultans' *tughras*.

As a result of the Islamic prohibition of figurative representation, the ornament, which was previously used as a simple decorative accessory, took on a central role. An emphasis on geometric and vegetal motifs is already in evidence in the Dome of the Rock in Jerusalem, as the ornament was gradually becoming the main design element used in a sacred context. It can be seen in the extensive stucco reliefs decorating the interior walls of the Dome of the Rock, as well as in many other buildings. Flower and foliage tendrils were the favorite theme. They were not depicted in a naturalistic way, but intertwined with each other in a stylized, geometric fashion. This vegetal decoration, the arabesque, spread from Baghdad throughout the whole of the Islamic world during the 10th century and in Iran in particular, was taken to masterful levels.

Above:
Tiles with 12-pointed stars in the Hall of the Ambassadors
Alhambra, Comares Palace (Granada), 14th century

Intertwined stars, which symbolize cosmic harmony, are a common theme on tiles.

Below:
Cupola of the Gur-i Mir Mausoleum in Samarqand
(Uzbekistan), end of the 14th–beginning of the 15th century

Left:
Detail of the façade
Great Mosque of Córdoba, 785–988 CE

The design of the Mezquita's façade is an example of the use of vegetal and ornamental surface patterns from the early period of Islamic architecture. Above the decorative columns set into the wall are white and red stone arches similar to the ones that surmount the so-called forest of columns in the interior of the mosque.

Islamic Law

Owing to its practical outlook, Islam as a social framework possesses a highly developed legal system (*sharia*), which embraces nearly every aspect of daily life. As with religious matters, the written sources of this law are the Qur'an and the *hadiths*. At the heart of the administration of justice is the Islamic conception of man being free to choose between good and evil and bearing responsibility for his own deeds.

The classical schools of law—four Sunni and one Shiite—to whom the faithful could turn when they needed help, developed as early as the 9th century. The *sharia*, which is supposed to foster ethical conduct in all areas of life, concentrates particularly on inheritance and family law, but also pays attention to the social issues important to the faith, such as the prohibition of usury and monopolies. In addition, it details the various forms of physical punishment, for which extremely high standards of evidence are required. In general, the *sharia* is highly flexible, and recognizes both exceptions and expiation.

The interior of a library, 1237
Miniature by al-Wasiti
Paris, Bibliothèque Nationale

Believers, conduct yourselves with justice and bear true witness before God, even though it be against yourselves, your parents, or your kinsfolk. Be they rich or poor, God knows better about them both. So do not be led by passion, lest you swerve from the truth. If you distort it, know that God is cognizant of all your actions.

Sura 4, 135

Opposite:
Qur'an students in front of the portal of the Kalan Mosque in Bukhara, Uzbekistan

A group of mullahs in the courtyard of the Imam Raza Mosque in Mashhad, Iran

Qur'an and the Sunna

In addition to forming the religious foundations of Islam, the Qur'an and the Sunna ("custom") are also the two sources of law for the proper conduct of Muslims in everyday life. Historically, this model of proper conduct was established on the one hand by the early ordinances decreed by Muhammad following the flight to Medina, which dealt essentially with legal questions, while on the other by the *hadiths*, most of which date from the Medina period. In these the Prophet gives his opinion on legal and everyday questions.

The precedence over religious dogma given to the rules of proper conduct and the behavior of the community is given particularly

clear expression in the Islamic legal system, the *sharia*. Islam does not presuppose any separation between religious and everyday life. The *sharia* is not, therefore, a system of laws based simply on the religious obligations of the faith, but should be seen instead as a complete set of instructions for leading an ethical

Qur'an school in Yemen

The traditional Qur'an school, attended by boys from the age of seven, not only teaches knowledge of the Qur'an, but also the flawless recitation of its suras. Great importance is attached to this as a way of instilling in the Muslim an enduring attachment to his roots. Within the framework of a campaign to combat illiteracy (particularly in country areas) that was conducted after the Second World War, Qur'an schools were largely replaced by elementary schools for pupils of both sexes.

Mustansiriya Madrasa in Baghdad, 1232

This *madrasa*, built shortly before the Mongol invasion, was once one of the most important Islamic universities. Since the *madrasa* system developed by the Seljuks had become the main form of teaching institute under the orthodox Sunni establishment, not only were theologians and jurists educated here, but also the empire's future administrative elite.

life in all spheres. Many scholars therefore equate Islam with *sharia*: Islamic law serves as a unifying bond between all Muslims across the world.

As a lay religion, Islam does not have "theologians" in a Christian sense, but legal scholars whose position is similar in that they provide the faithful with practical help in cases of confusion or doubt. Muslims—individuals as well as communities or governments—present the legal scholar or jurist with their questions, whereupon the jurist issues a legal opinion (*fatwa*) whose contents he is responsible for, and whose decisions the petitioners then comply with.

In addition to the Qur'an and the Sunna as sources of law, the *sharia* can also recognize two other, more "technical," methods in the running of legal questions: this can be settlement by analogy, whereby the judgment from one case is applied to another, similar case; and also settlement by jurists' consensus, whereby a particular case is examined by a committee of legal scholars. The principle behind the latter is that while a single jurist might make a mistake, God in His goodness would not allow the whole community to err. Islamic law is thus distinctive for its high degree of flexibility, and is sophisticated in terms of the many different methods of compensation and expiation it allows. Furthermore, throughout the Islamic world, elements of the local law of custom that once prevailed in a particular region have also been adopted into Islamic law.

Two scholars, 1229 Syrian miniature Istanbul, Topkapi Palace Library

Islamic jurists base their judgments on the Qur'an and the *hadiths*, as God, who transmitted His laws to His Messenger Muhammad so that the order of creation could be upheld, is the sole lawgiver.

Their knowledge of the sources and legal tradition allows the legal scholars to decide whether an analogy can be drawn with a known case or whether a particular situation requires a new judgment. The criterion used is always consistent with the teachings of Muhammad.

The flexibility of the legal principles of Islam stems from the idea that perfect Islamic law could only operate in a perfect community. As this is not the case, a legal "state of emergency" is in force in which "innovative decisions" have to be admitted.

Principles of Islamic Law

Islamic law unites juristic ideas with ethical-religious ideas. Orthodox Islam starts from the assumption that man, using his power of reason, can distinguish good deeds from bad. He has laws to obey and duties to perform with respect to God—essentially the Five Pillars of Islam—as well as towards his fellow man. Islamic law claims to be able to regulate all human behavior through laws and prohibitions. The function of the state in this process is to make sure the law is applied without intruding upon the creation of law.

Human behavior can be divided into five categories:

1. Obligatory acts or duties, the performance of which is rewarded by God and the omission of which is punished by God.

2. Recommended or desirable acts, which are beneficial to the members of the community. The performance of these is rewarded; their omission, however, is not reproached nor is it punished.

Execution of an infidel in North Africa
Copperplate engraving

Physical punishments are described in the Qur'an, but are nevertheless subject to strict rules. In the case of premeditated killing or physical injury, the victim's next of kin—or the victim himself—can demand a similar punishment for the perpetrator of the crime. Licentious behavior or adultery, crimes which are punishable by flogging or stoning, must have been witnessed by four men.

Judges, 1237
Miniature by al-Wasiti
Paris, Bibliothèque Nationale

A judge in the Islamic system of law, *sharia*, has far-reaching responsibilities. As well as settling disputes between the faithful and examining witnesses, he must also perform notarial and tutelary duties. Today, *sharia* courts are responsible for marriage, family and inheritance law, as well as the administration of the religious foundations. Previously, judges were appointed by the ruler, to whom they were answerable, primarily regarding the observance of religious rules governing public life. They were subordinate to a court presided over by the ruler or his vizier, which could overturn disputed verdicts and settle particularly difficult or politically delicate cases. They also investigated the misuse of power by the authorities and irregularities in the collection of taxes.

3. Allowable acts that are ethically neutral and left to the judgment of the individual.

4. Undesirable or reprehensible acts, the avoidance of which is rewarded while their performance is not punished.

5. Forbidden acts, the avoidance of which is imperative and is rewarded, and the performance of which is reproached and punished.

Since all laws are seen as having been decreed by God, their contravention is regarded as the flouting of the just world order and as ingratitude toward the Creator. However, every law has its own set of alleviation procedures, exceptions or substitute acts. Thus certain religious obligations, such as fasting, can be postponed until a later time.

Man's sins are classified into three groups: the worst are those against God and the religion; followed by those against fellow men and their right to freedom from injury; finally there are those relating to everyday matters such as offenses against property, damage to the reputation of another, and bearing false witness.

According to the Qur'an, God can forgive man all his sins, should He so choose, except the sin of lack of faith. Man does not become an unbeliever as a result of contravening individual laws or duties, but only by denying the binding nature of the commandments.

Algerian Qadi (judge) at work photograph taken 1936

Judges are able to settle many cases relating to everyday life to the advantage of the faithful by imposing expiatory measures, invoking the rules of exception or employing "legal tricks." For abandoned wives or pregnant widows, for example, there is the "sleeping fetus" rule, whereby a child can be recognized as the rightful heir to the deceased or absent husband five or even seven years later.

The Classical Law Schools

The four classical Sunni schools of law, which still exist today, developed during the eighth and ninth centuries within the framework of a comprehensive legal codification of human behavior.

1. The Hanafi school, named after its founder Abu Hanifa (699–767 CE), is the largest, oldest and most liberal of the law schools, and leaves abundant scope for the use of reason. As the school of law adopted by the Abbasids and the Ottomans, it is today the established school in their successor states, and also in much of Central Asia, Pakistan and India.

Around one-third of all Muslims follow the Hanafi school of thought.

2. The Maliki school, named after Malik ibn Anas (715–795 CE), is more conservative and strongly oriented toward the law of custom practiced in Medina during the time of the Prophet. This school of law is predominant in the Maghreb, North Africa, the Sudan and Kuwait.

3. The Shafii school, named after al-Shafii (767–820 CE), occupies the middle ground between the first two schools, and is followed in Jordan, Palestine, Egypt, and Southeast Asia.

4. The Hanbali school, named after Ahmed ibn Hanbal (780–855 CE), represents an extreme form of conservative traditionalism, which is why it is mainly followed by small

Wooden board from Nigeria containing a Qur'anic inscription in Arabic
Berlin, Museum of Ethnology

These wooden boards are used in schools for the teaching of the Qur'an.

Inner courtyard of the Al-Azhar Mosque, 970–972 CE
Cairo, Egypt

The Al-Azhar Mosque, with the *madrasa* that adjoins it, is Egypt's major university, and the leading teaching institute of the Sunni branch of Islam. It therefore hands down legal opinions, primarily in response to appeals by governments which often have far-reaching consequences. For a long time its orientation was contested. However, a few years ago a moderate and more open-minded leadership managed to take control.

Qur'an school, 1902
Oil painting by
Rudolph Ernst
Private collection

During Islam's early period, characterized by a philosophical outlook, legal scholars had to prove they were capable of making their own independently reasoned legal judgments (*ijtihad* or "struggling on one's own"). This principle stems from the high value placed on the human faculty of reason. The principle of "endurance" was equally important, whereby a certainty once established would remain valid until it was proved incorrect. This also means that as a matter of principle, actions were permissible until expressly forbidden. In the 11th century, Sunni Islam witnessed a "closing of the gate" regarding *ijtihad* in favor of legal dogma, while the Shiites rejected this "closing of the gate" and continued to attach great importance to the independent efforts of their jurists—even to the extent of rejecting the practice of invoking legal precedents with the phrase: "The dead have nothing to say."

communities in Syria, Algeria, Iraq and Afghanistan. It remains powerful, however, as the official, established school of Saudi Arabia.

Unlike the Sunni schools, the Shiite school of law has, since the 11th–12th centuries, recognized only independent legal rulings. It believes that every case should be judged on its own merits and that jurists should produce their own judgment, rather than referring to verdicts that have been delivered in similar cases.

Islamic Law in Everyday Life

During his time in Medina, Muhammad gave his opinion on legal questions relating to everyday situations—for example, on the stipulations of a marriage contract or divorce, or the guardianship of orphans. Right up to the present day, therefore, family and inheritance law have always played a significant role within the *sharia* legal system. The giving of alms, the third pillar of Islam, which was expanded into a precisely formulated system of taxation, and rules concerning gifts and religious foundations, were also fixed during this early period. The community was always concerned to support its weaker members of society— women, widows, children and orphans. Full legal responsibility in Islam is granted to adults in possession of all their mental faculties, although limited legal responsibility begins with birth. For this reason, rules concerning guardianship and other dependent relationships are extremely important. The judge (*qadi*), who settles the believers' legal problems and disputes locally, is also responsible for the administration of the wealth of private and princely foundations. He is also guardian to foundlings, the mentally ill, and certain other minors. Previously the market overseer was also answerable to the judge, which meant he had ultimate responsibility for maintaining public order, observing prayer times, and dress regulations as well as for trading matters.

The Ban on Profiteering

The well-known Islamic ban on charging interest, or profiteering—a feature of Muslims' everyday life—is connected to the religious and legal stipulations regarding taxation and the social obligations that accompany property ownership. These require that profit resulting from possession should be shared with the weaker members of society. However, whether the term "riba" (from raba, meaning "to multiply") used in the Qur'an refers to all forms of interest or only profiteering *per se* is still a matter of dispute today. In any event, Muslims frequently used to leave their financial transactions to the Jews, Christians or Hindus, and to a certain extent still do. As a rule, western practices prevail in Islamic banking today, although in the stricter Islamic states a system of profit-sharing by the lender in place of payment of interest by the debtor or the concealing of interest as "operational charges" is common. Greed, showing-off and miserliness, as well as money-hoarding, speculation and the formation of monopolies, are considered sinful. Sura 9 threatens those who hoard gold and silver, instead of spending it, with a particular form of torment in hell: they are branded with coins heated in hell's fire. The complicated *sharia*

Algerian Qadi at work
photograph, ca. 1936

Algerian women at the open window of a Qadi's office, photograph taken around 1936

inheritance law, which limits the share received by individuals and takes into account the many claims likely to be made by various (male) relatives, is also designed to avoid these particular sins. It therefore hinders the concentration of wealth in the hands of one person.

Physical Punishments

Muhammad had successfully curbed the ancient Arab blood revenge customs, replacing them with strict physical punishments as laid down by the *sharia*. The best known of these are the amputation of limbs as a punishment (and possibly a deterrent) for theft, and the stoning of female adulterers. Such drastic measures show that, while sexuality is approved in Islamic society, it is also subject to strict rules, transgression of which, particularly by women, is severely and violently punished. Physical punishments in all their harshness are today still applied in a small number of Islamic states, such as Saudi Arabia and Pakistan, and to a more limited extent in Sudan and Libya.

The *Sharia* Today

The extent of the *sharia*'s influence is a major issue for Islamists today. In most Islamic states, particularly those with a colonial past or clear modern outlook, the validity of the *sharia* is limited to family, religious and local issues affecting the life of a village or city community. State law has been brought into line with that of Europe or comprises a hybrid of European and Islamic elements. Certain countries, particularly Turkey, but also Tunisia, Algeria and Syria, have undertaken a far-reaching secularization of their legal systems, which is seen by Islamists as an alienation and suppression of the original law, which was designed to lead the believer to salvation. They are therefore calling forcefully for the reintroduction of ancient *sharia* law. Against this comes the argument that *sharia* law was always influenced by the law of custom that existed in the different Islamic regions. The *sharia* has therefore never existed as an independent abstract system.

Funeral in Karachi
Pakistan

Family and Society

Islamic culture was originally rooted in the culture of the Arab lands, which were dominated by nomadic family and clan relationships. However, the Prophet Muhammad succeeded in dismantling the ancient tribal rivalries and replacing them with a common faith.

Family and marriage came to enjoy a privileged position within Islam, with the polygamy of former times soon largely eradicated. The bond of marriage became an agreement based on contractual law, supported by certain social safeguards. Muhammad attempted at an early stage to improve the legal status of women, which had been shrouded in notions of religious taboo. Many aspects of discrimination that persisted could therefore be ascribed to the prevailing law of custom rather than to religion.

Islam emphasized the equality of all believers before God, but considerable social differences existed during the early period, particularly between town and country. In terms of economic organization, Islam approved of private property but subjected it to a number of social obligations.

Coffee house, Damascus, Syria

The Prophet said: "A faithful believer to a faithful believer is like the bricks of a wall, enforcing each other." While saying that, the Prophet clasped his hands by interlacing his fingers.

He sat with us still when a man approached and asked for alms. The Prophet turned to us and said: "Give to him and you will be rewarded for your gift! And God fulfils what he promises through his Prophet!"

Hadith narrated by Abu Musa

Opposite:
Muslim wedding in Makassar/Sulawesi, Indonesia

Carpet sellers in Samarqand, Uzbekistan

Clans and Guilds

Muhammad's life was dominated by the alliances and enmities of the Arab clans. In Medina, however, he was successful in uniting his fellow tribesmen into a cross-clan community, worshipping one God and one religion. But the rules of clan affinity and the organization of tribal groups still play an important role throughout the whole Islamic world, in particular in the Arab heartlands. They are the rules of desert dwellers who had to survive in a barren and hostile environment and were therefore primarily concerned with control of territory, oases and caravans. They also related to rights of water extraction and tribute payments for the right to cross land held by a different tribe. Even Muhammad made use of polygamy in order to marry into influential neighboring tribes and

Qashqai tribes in Iran
The nomadic tribes are usually classified according to the type of livestock they keep: the term "Bedouin" refers to dromedary-herding horseback warriors. The religious customs of the Islamic Bedouins still include a number of pre-Islamic elements.

Nomads in Oman
Although Islam is largely an urban culture, nomads, who are organized into clans and whose relationship with the cities remains a tense one, have always played an important role in Islamic belief.

forge alliances with them. The early Arab social system can be described as a patriarchal "tribal democracy": high-powered political leaders distributed rights and privileges among members of their own clan, and thus, as a result of common interest and the equitable division of wealth, secured their loyalty. Since the Qur'an exhorts the faithful to consult with others, and some rulers adopted the practice of holding regular councils (*shura*), Islamist apologists see this "*shura* democracy" as an early form of parliamentary system. The Saudi Arabian king is still surrounded today by a diet of 6000 princes of his house who each hold important public office and dispose of vast sums of wealth. The power of large ruling families can also be seen in the non-monarchical states—for example, Libya and Syria, where the office of president has become hereditary.

Similar to clan loyalty is the system of client relationships, the direct political, social or financial dependency of certain individuals or groups of individuals on the powerful and wealthy, to whom they owe personal loyalty in return. This

situation is also en   the fact that Islamic *sh*   not recognize the co   al entity"—for examp   es. Although nearly   ic country today has organizations of this type, such as unions, their influence is still exerted by means of personal agreements and arrangements, which significantly hinders the development of a "class consciousness" or of solidarity between the affected parties.

However, one type of federal organization is in evidence in the case of city craftsmen and merchants, who started forming guilds as early as the 8th century. The main purpose of these was to provide social safeguards (for example, old age provision) and for communal services within the different types of trade. In every major Islamic city there were hundreds of guilds. The city of

Turkish traders in a bazaar, photograph taken around 1885

Traders, who mainly sell their goods from small shops, are still organized into guilds today.

The Dyers' Souk in Fez, Morocco

The dyers and tanners belong to one of the less well-respected types of trade, and are located in the outer area of the market. In the Maghreb and other regions, cloths and fabrics are still dyed in the traditional way today. This involves bare-legged workers standing in the stone tubs containing natural or artificial dyes in order to full the fabric.

Istanbul alone possessed over 1000 during the 17th century. The guilds administered funds to which all their members contributed and upon which they could call for loans or other support as required. The different trades also paid for services such as armed protection, night-watchmen or cleaners for their own district of the city, and financed their own festivals and processions out of their guild funds. An elected leader would maintain contact with the ruler, as the guilds were not self-governing political bodies, but had to come to an arrangement with the city authorities.

Marriage and Family

The Qur'an and the *hadiths* emphatically encourage Muslims to marry and procreate—unlike Christianity, Islam does not view celibacy as commendable in any religious sense. In Islam the family enjoys a privileged position and, as in many other religions, is considered the cornerstone of society. The private sphere is strongly protected. Therefore, in private houses the family's living area is not visible from the entrance area in which visitors are entertained.

Traditionally, Islam used to promote marriage between related parties, in order to keep economic property within the extended family. Marriage is treated as a legal institution and is negotiated contractually, thus offering many opportunities for improving the position of women. According to the Qur'an, a man may take a maximum of four wives, but only if they are cared for and treated equally. In reality, though, the practice of polygamy has been abolished by law in nearly all Islamic countries. Nowadays, most marriage contracts contain a clause giving the woman power to refuse her husband

Wedding scene in India

The Islamic marriage ceremony is a contract in civil law involving mutual promises and is carried out before witnesses in a judge's office. The contract is often negotiated beforehand by the two families. Weddings are celebrated in a highly festive manner and can last several days. This is the marriage of a respected Sufi in India.

permission to take a second wife. The practice of divorce, which for a long time only provided for the one-sided repudiation of the wife by the husband (in front of witnesses), has now, in most countries, been regulated, to ensure that all divorce cases take place in a courtroom, making it easier for women to initiate divorce. In general, however, marriage is seen as a bond blessed by God and divorce as something abhorred by God.

Birth control is not uniformly regulated throughout Islam. As for abortion, while the traditional schools of law allowed it during the first four months, there is a widespread belief today that only God has the right to make a decision over life and death. Risk to the mother's life, though, is widely seen as a justifiable reason for abortion.

Celebration at the court of the Mughal emperor Akbar on the birth of his son Salim, 1603–1605
Indian miniature

Large feasts were held at rulers' courts to celebrate the birth of a son. Akbar the Great (1556–1605) held a series of celebrations lasting several weeks when his son Salim, who used the name Jahangir when he succeeded his father, was born. Even today, the birth of a son confers improved social standing on Muslims; in many regions, children are the only guarantee of being looked after during their old age.

Persian harem scene, 17th century
Cairo, National Library

The word "harem" (which derives from the Arabic word *harim*, meaning a "consecrated, inviolable place") denotes the main the living quarters of women and children, which was inaccessible to visitors. At the court of rulers such as the Ottomans, the harem area could encompass several thousand individuals.

Following the act of naming, children are regarded as independent beings who are both under the protection of the community and required to learn its rules. Bringing up children is traditionally the domain of women, with the wider family expected to lend a hand. Children attend school from the age of seven; traditional Qur'an schools, which used to be for boys only, have been replaced by mixed state schools in nearly all Islamic countries. Coming of age is set by Islam at between 13 and 15 years old, and, for young men in particular, this time of their lives is associated with the assumption of full religious obligations.

The Role of Women

It is true that you have certain rights with regard to your women, but they also have rights over you.

Hadith

Woman at a loom in Egypt

In terms of religion, women are full members of the Muslim community. God's revelation is directed specifically at both sexes, and there are no privileges awarded to men where salvation is concerned. But the word *harim* (harem), denoting the area of a house reserved for women, has the same root as *haram*, the "holy area," where "holy" is equated with "forbidden." This indicates that the women's area is taboo for visitors. In addition, because of the female menstrual cycle, women have been seen as impure, a notion adopted from Judaism. It should be stressed, however, that the Prophet Muhammad significantly improved the lot of women in the Arab lands. He opposed the ancient Arabian custom of polygamy, established the duty of Muslim men to pay maintenance to their women, and gave women control over a portion of their wealth as well as the right of inheritance. In West Africa and Southeast Asia there are matriarchal societies that retained their matriarchal structure even after adopting Islam and have survived to the present day. However, Islam also adopted discriminatory rules and practices from the traditional law of custom of many different countries. One example of this is female circumcision in Africa, which is practiced in certain Muslim and Christian societies. This has no basis in either the Qur'an or the *hadiths*, but simply stems from traditional local practice.

There are also rules that discriminate against women in the *sharia*. For example, a Muslim man is allowed to marry a non-Muslim woman, but Muslim women are not permitted to marry non-Muslim men. In addition, it is considered justifiable for men to beat

Muhammad, his daughter Fatima, his favorite wife Aisha, and his wife Umm Salama, 1595
Turkish miniature
Dublin, Chester Beatty Library

their wives under certain circumstances. Here, though, Islam also grants women certain exclusive rights of inviolability, which are not shared by men. Feminists and modernizers are fighting primarily for an end to male guardianship of women, for equal rights before the law, and for the abolition of the compulsory wearing of the veil. The guardianship laws include the practice of marrying off women by the head of the family, even against their will, despite the fact that the Qur'an grants women the right to choose their own spouses.

A related issue is the fight against women being confined to the home. All modern Islamic states encourage the participation of women in the life of society, and there have therefore been, or currently are, women in leading positions or even female heads of Islamic government (for example in Bangladesh) in all Islamic countries, with the exception of certain states on the Arabian Peninsula. The lack of equality before the law affects women's status as witnesses and the law of inheritance, but most countries have already taken legal steps to remedy this. In particular, women have been forced to fight a long battle to secure control over their rightful share of inheritance, which often remained under the supervision and administration of the male-dominated extended family. The veil is one of the most familiar controversial issues affecting women today. Although it had already existed in ancient Arab cultures, by the time of the Prophet it no longer played an important role. The Qur'an and the *sharia* require women to cover

Veiled Muslim student in a biology lab in Cairo

Fashion show in Istanbul

themselves from the neck to the ankles and below the elbows, but not to cover their faces. These requirements are met precisely by the *chador* (tent) worn in Iran. The veiling of the face—also practiced by Bedouin men—or wearing of head coverings that leave only a slit for vision, have predominantly magical origins, whereby women, particularly pregnant women, were supposed to protect themselves against the evil eye and against demons penetrating through their facial orifices. The veil, introduced at the end of the 8th century, a time when the Persian influence over Islamic culture was growing, was an item of urban dress that indicated the elevated status of the lady of the house (who did not do any physical work), whereas the servants and workers

would wear a head scarf at the most. Furthermore, it was also supposed to prevent a show of beauty, youth, pregnancy or make-up, which might arouse envy and thus provoke molestation or interference. The compulsory wearing of the veil demanded by Islamists today aims to subjugate women to traditional rules and gender roles. Many younger Muslim women in a non-Islamic environment, on the other hand, deliberately choose to wear the veil or head scarf as a way of demonstrating their Islamic identity. This is widespread among young Islamic women living in Europe. As a general rule, Islamic women have been battling to win more rights and greater equality within the Muslim community, rather than battling against the religion. Since the end of the First World War there have been women's rights movements in most Islamic countries, following the first legal reforms in favor of women, which were pushed through in 1915. Many legal scholars hold the view that everyday discrimination against women, though existent in most Islamic societies today, has its roots not in Islam but in earlier social structures, and should have no place in today's world or in a modernized *sharia*.

Social Structure

Islam defines man as a social being and the Islamic *Ummah* as the best kind of community, because it believes in God. The community represents an intermediate stage between God and the individual. God's revelation calls for the active ordering of the world, and Islamic society, in its ideal form, is a "theonomy": God is the sole lawgiver and true ruler; all temporal authority receives its legitimation from Him alone and is duty bound to enforce His laws. The rule of men must, therefore, never become an end in itself, which is why Islam does not identify with ideas regarding absolute autonomy and the sovereignty of mankind. The declaration

Door knocker
Morocco

Among the countless practices of popular Islam which still play an important role, primarily in rural areas, is a belief in the protective power of amulets. Door knockers and pendants in the shape of the "hand of Fatima," whose five fingers are regarded as lucky charms, are commonly found in Morocco. They are associated with the healing powers of the Prophet's daughter, and can also be seen as a step towards feminine emancipation.

Allahu akbar (God is greater) is designed to continually exhort all Muslim men to be modest. The overall good of the community takes priority over that of the individual. Although Islam expressly approves of private property, all forms of ownership place an obligation upon the owners to share their wealth.

In spite of the fundamental principle of the equality of all Muslims, Islamic society was dominated by the Arabs during its early period. However, with the rapid campaigns of conquest and the rise of the cities with their different population groups came a reduction in the privileges enjoyed by the Arab ruling class, and the advancement of other peoples and their traditions. In the Maghreb, though, there still exists a cultural and social contrast between the poor Berber populations in the south and the wealthier populations of immigrant Arab descent in the north—this is just one example of similar differences encountered elsewhere in the Islamic world. On the whole, Islam is an

Manufacture of air-dried bricks in the region of Luxor,
Egypt

The difference between city and country reveals itself in the different working methods employed. While most cities contain modern districts housing office blocks and banks, in country areas even the simplest tools are often lacking. Agriculture and traditional handcrafts are often practiced in exactly the same way today as they were 100 or even several 100 years ago.

urbanized culture, and the social differences between city and country are pronounced in some Islamic nations.

Apart from the ruling elite, the highest social position in Islam is occupied by the *ulema*, a collective term for all Qur'an scholars. On the lowest rung of the hierarchy are the day laborers. There are Muslims who can trace their lineage directly back to the Prophet's grandsons, Hassan and Hussein, and they enjoy particularly high religious prestige, and carry the honorary title *sharif* ("high-born individual") for descendants of Hassan, and *sayyid* ("lord, master") for descendants of Hussein. In some countries these individuals receive a state income. In the case of the Shiites, similar respect is also owed to those Muslims who can claim descent from the imams.

Above:
Wafi Shopping Center, Dubai

The immense wealth generated by the export of petroleum has led, above all in the United Arab Emirates (to which Dubai belongs), to the creation of modern cities. The shopping arcades often exceed western standards and their cleanliness gives the impression of deliberate contrast with the traditional bazaars.

Below, left:
The Maidan
Isfahan, Iran

After establishing Isfahan as his capital, Abbas the Great (1587–1629) set about building the central "king's square" (Maidan-i Shah) on which the splendid Shah Mosque and Sheikh Lutfallah Mosque stand. The main purpose of the square was to serve as a parade ground for demonstrations of the ruler's power. The leading guilds, among them the wealthy carpet-sellers guild, which still plays an important role today, also moved into premises around its edges. In the areas beyond the main square lived the craftsmen transported from the Caucasus in separate districts according to their trade.

Trade and Economy

Merchants and tradesmen possess high status in Islam. On the one hand, Mecca and Medina, the cities in which Muhammad was active, were important trading centers, and on the other, the Prophet himself was a caravan leader and traveling merchant before he was called by God. Another reason is that the ancient trading routes, such as the "Incense Route" had been the lifelines of the Arab cultural region since time immemorial. Maintaining these trading routes was the most important duty of rulers and the mightiest princes were considered to be those whose lands were safe for traders to travel through. Large caravanserais were built along the trading routes. These often resembled small cities in the desert, including accommodation

View of Constantinople
1819
Copperplate engraving

Constantinople was a vital Islamic center for the trade between Asia and Europe.

Abu Zayd traveling by ship, 1236–1237
Miniature from the *Maqamat* of al-Hariri, Baghdad
Paris, Bibliothèque Nationale

The crafty hero of the *Maqamat* of al-Hariri (1054–1122) loses his entire worldly possessions in this exciting story. Banished and forced to undertake a journey, he repeatedly acquires money through his skills as businessman and trader, but always manages to lose it again.

for rent, rooms in which business could be conducted, guest-houses and their own markets.

This long-distance trading resulted in a wide variety of wares being made available in the cities. Just as the Mosque forms its religious center, the bazaar represents the secular center of the city. It is not only a place for the transaction of business, however, but also for meeting people and exchanging information, as evidenced

Gold coin with Kufi inscription, 1125
Granada
Berlin, Museum of Islamic Art

Islam adopted the use of coinage from the Byzantine empire.

Almohad dirham
12th–13th centuries
Madrid, Museo Arqueológico

The most common types of coinage, the dinar and the dirham, are still used in various countries today.

by the lengthy rituals of greeting and haggling. As a public space, the bazaar was traditionally a male domain.

The bazaar has always been under the strict control of a market overseer and to some degree still is today. It is easily lockable and in the past had its own troops for protection. It does not merely consist of shops and stalls, but also forms the veritable "heart of the city" accommodating workshops and storerooms, offices, coffee houses, restaurants and public baths. Common to all bazaars is the grouping of different types of trade into their own streets and alleyways, arranged according to proximity to the Mosque: the inner ring is taken up by "clean" wares such as spices, perfume, books and jewelry; then come the textiles, household goods

Courtyard of a *funduq* ("hotel" for traders), Morocco

The quarters for traders and traveling businessmen have inner courtyards where goods are inspected before being bought and sold.

Silk merchants' bazaar in Cairo
1838/39
Chalk lithograph by David Roberts

All Islamic towns/urban areas possess magnificent bazaars, which are usually roofed or else comprise individual market halls. The silk merchants have one of the most highly respected and wealthiest guilds, which finances the equipping of its section of the bazaar to the standard required in order to impress its customers with a display of sheer luxury.

and food traders' alleyways, while the "unclean" trades such as dyers, tanners, butchers and blacksmiths form the outer ring. As trade is organized in Islam along largely private lines, in the towns and cities it is usually a small economic elite who own the majority of goods, means of production, shops and storerooms. The smaller traders and farmers are often indebted to them as a result of large credits they have taken, or else lease the right to use their property from them. In a system of "income capitalism," the elite live on the repayments made by their debtors. Through its system of social obligations, Islam exerts pressure on the economic elite to use their profits to finance social projects such as hospitals, soup kitchens or religious foundations.

Until relatively recently, the towns and cities were not politically self-governing, but directly dependent on the ruler or city authorities. Most rulers participated in free trade, just like any other private individuals.

Cultural Self-Contemplation

At the heart of Islamic rule is the concept of theocracy, the sole rule by God, Who is just. However, over the course of time a multiplicity of different political systems has developed in the Muslim world. The ongoing contact with the West, which began with the colonial era, represents a challenge for many Islamic governments. Following the emergence of various political movements such as nationalism and socialism, most governments promote modernization in the scientific, technical and educational spheres, while retaining a skeptical attitude toward the loss of religion and the change in values that have occurred during the second half of the 20th century.

This period and the beginning of the 21st century have also seen the rise of Islamist groups, who oppose westernization and fight instead for strict Islamic rule. In some countries these groups—based in part on a reduction of the term *jihad*, meaning "armed holy war"— have become increasingly militant and more of an obstacle to the modernization efforts of Islamic countries, as well as to cultural globalization. The more extreme Islamist groups have committed acts of global terrorism as part of their *jihad*, and anti-western intentions.

View of the city of Abu Dhabi, United Arab Emirates

Islam enjoys the distinction of not being bound up with one specific person or one specific people. The word "Islam" does not signify this kind of relationship, as it denotes no man, people or country. It is not an invention of the human intellect and does not limit itself to a particular community. Islam is a world-embracing religion whose purpose is to generate and cultivate Islamic qualities and attitudes in people's minds. Strictly speaking, Islam is an adjective. To whomever this adjective applies, of whatever race or community, land or people, he is a Muslim. As is written in the Qur'an, every nation and every period has known good, upright individuals who fit this description; they were and are all Muslims.

Sayyid Abu-i-ala Maudoodi (1903–1979)

Opposite:
Muslim at prayer; in the background is a butane gas tank
photograph taken around 1950

Mosque of Hassan II in Casablanca
Morocco

Islamic Political Systems

For all Muslims, the period of rule by Muhammad, and for the Sunnis, that of the Four Rightly Guided Caliphs (632–661 CE) to which the principle of a dynastic succession was attached, represent the perfect model for a just and fair political system. However, the Shiites reject this principle, believing that the "rule of kings" is incompatible with the divinely inspired leadership of the imams.

The concept of "theocracy" was supposed to restrict the power of some men over others. This led to the political order of the Islamic world continually being challenged by revolutionaries, usually Shiite movements,

who disputed the legitimacy of the current regime and wanted to precipitate the return of the Mahdi, the just ruler who, they believe, will appear at the end of time.

Ever since the end of the colonial era, political rule in Islam has been forced to face technical, scientific and economic challenges of the modern age, and has often found itself caught between the preservation of

Sheikhs in Dubai
United Arab Emirates

The great wealth of Saudi Arabia, Kuwait, Brunei, and the Emirates of the Persian Gulf, which allows many of their inhabitants a life of luxury free from taxation, is based on the export of petroleum. Since the sale of production concessions to the USA and Europe at the beginning of the 20th century, oil has become a political factor. The petroleum-producing countries look after their interests through the Organization of Petroleum Exporting Countries (OPEC), founded in 1960.

King Hassan II of Morocco
(1929–1999)

Morocco combines a traditional monarchy with a parliament that includes opposing groups. Hassan II, who had been king since 1960, has pursued a moderate foreign policy, while ruling at home (and having survived several assassination attempts) in a more autocratic style. In 1976 he undertook the "Green March" and annexed Western Sahara.

Gamal Abdel Nasser and Yasser Arafat
Photograph taken around 1970

The Palestine region became a trouble spot in 1948 after the proclamation of the state of Israel. When Arafat became leader of the Palestine Liberation Organization in 1969, the conflict intensified. In the 1950s, President Nasser of Egypt headed Arab opposition to Israel, but whereas he supported the armed conflict of the Palestinians, his successor, Anwar Sadat, changed course, pursuing a policy of rapprochement.

traditional values and subscribing to the globalized society. The political legacy of the colonial powers consisted of government institutions fashioned in the European image—for example, the division of the political machinery into ministerial departments—but there is a tendency among the individual leaders of Islamic countries to exert a dominating influence over their political structures. The parliaments, a feature of nearly all Islamic countries, therefore vary widely in terms of the degree of power they hold.

On the whole, Islamic countries do not have a problem with the idea of a constitution, as Muhammad's ordinances in Medina provide a model for this. The first modern constitutions in the Islamic world were introduced in Tunisia (1861)

and Egypt (1866). The repression of traditional Islamic power structures, in particular the *sharia*, led to modernization everywhere, but also in some places to a strengthening of centralized power, which sometimes took on dictatorial dimensions due to the lack of any form of control over the ruler.

Today a variety of forms of government exist: alongside traditional monarchies (Morocco, Kuwait) are modern, moderate presidential governments (Tunisia). In many countries (Pakistan, Algeria) the military plays a decisive role; the authoritarian regime once characterized by clan rule (Iraq) has ended with the overthrow of Saddam Hussein by the US military in 2005. A special form of government holds power in the Shiite cleric-dominated Republic of Iran.

Turkey

Turkey's political and religious life displays many unique features of its own, and provides a good illustration of the difficulties faced by modern Islamic countries in dealing with their own Islamic tradition. The fall of the Ottoman empire, the last of the large Islamic empires, was a gradual process that began in the early 19th century with the separation of Egypt and the European Balkan lands, the conflicts in the Arabian region, and conflict between the religious minorities. As a result of the disintegration of the empire—particularly the loss of the non-Muslim Balkan regions—the religious situation also changed. Whereas 20 percent of the empire's population had previously been non-Muslim, the proportion of non-Muslims in Turkey today is just 1 percent. During the First World War the empire fought on the side of Germany and Austria-Hungary, and was thus one of the political losers. The Treaty of Sèvres reduced Turkey to its current borders (Anatolia), thus taking away all of its imperial provinces. This situation led to a *coup*

d'état, unprecedented in the Islamic world, led by Mustafa Kemal Atatürk (1881–1938). President from 1923, Atatürk, supported by the military, undertook a radical modernization of all areas of life. He deposed the sultan, abolished *sharia* law, crushed the powerful religious orders, closed the *madrasas*, banned religious dress and the veil for women and, in 1928, pushed through a writing reform that involved the replacement of the Arabic alphabet with the Roman one, for religious use as well. By means of a form of authoritarian nationalism, Atatürk brought about a westernization of Turkish culture and forged close ties with Europe. He was supported in his efforts by the middle class population of the cities of western Turkey, while the hinterland

Pack mules in Anatolia

Kemal Atatürk (in white coat) (1881–1938) with Turkish diplomats in Ankara, Turkey, Photograph taken August 1922

was largely ignored. After Atatürk's death, the military in particular tried to separate Church from state, and reduce the influence of religion on public life (lay society). It also intervened in politics with several putsches (the last of these in 1980). Atatürk's political successors saw themselves confronted by a new Turkish religious and cultural identity, which they met with a variety of responses, ranging from tolerance to open sympathy. Cultural critics and scholars from the religious orders in particular found an audience in the Anatolian region as well as in the cities of western Turkey. Among other things they criticized the cultural lack of

Atatürk's daughter Ülkü Adatepe (left) in discussion with the sultan's granddaughter Hümeyra Özbaş, Kuşadasi, Turkey
Photograph taken 1998

Hagia Sophia in Istanbul
532–537 CE

direction, and the vacillation between Islamic tradition and the push for closer ties with the West, as well as the fact that the reforms had only benefited the population of the cities. These critics also increasingly started to reach the country's technical and scientific elite in addition to the losers in the one-sided modernization process. They also profited to a certain degree from the unresolved tensions with ethnic and religious minorities, such as the Kurds and the Shiite Alevites. The overall situation is far from transparent, however, as the Islamic authorities are more pluralistic in Turkey than elsewhere: there are convinced democrats who have succeeded in making Turkey a candidate to join the European Union, and who simply wish to reinforce Islam's role as an important element of the country's identity, but also opponents of reform who want to see the country turn away from the West and reintroduce *sharia* law. The Welfare Party, founded in 1970 by Necmettin Erbakan (prime minister 1996/97), the party to which many of Turkey's city mayors belong, has managed to exert a strong political influence in favor of increased Islamization. The lay parties want to fight Islam by democratic and parliamentary means, and resort to the outlawing of certain parties. However, they fear that this action will only succeed in driving them underground (where they will continue to operate, as in other countries). The Islamists' demands for greater social justice are likely to play an increasingly important role in politics in the future. On top of this, the lay politicians will also have to recognize that Islam, as part and parcel of the social structure of the country, cannot be banished from people's lives as easily as Atatürk might once have imagined.

Nationalism and Socialism

Europe's influence on the Islamic lands also extends to political concepts. Nationalism, for example, is a fundamentally alien concept within Islam, as the religion does not recognize borders between peoples and countries, emphasizing instead the equality of all Muslims. Nevertheless, nationalist ideas contributed to the anti-colonial liberation struggles and continue to play a part in the creation of a modern identity in most Islamic countries. Nationalism was also a banner for religious minorities who wanted to dispense with their status as protected peoples and claim equal civilian rights as members of the Arab community. Thus the founder of the Baath Party ("party of rebirth"), the ruling party in Syria and, formerly, Iraq, which propagates "Arab socialism" as well as nationalism, was the Syrian Christian Michel Aflaq.

The Egyptian president Gamal Abdel Nasser (1918–1970) in Cairo, shortly before the nationalization of the Suez Canal
Photograph taken on August 1, 1956

Charismatic President Nasser attracted a loyal following among Arabs like no other political leader. While domestically he pursued a socialist modernization policy and eliminated the Islamist threat, in terms of Egypt's foreign policy he displayed self-confidence by nationalizing the Suez Canal, which precipitated an international crisis.

Hafez al-Assad, president of Syria (1928–2000)
Photograph taken 1976

Assad seized power in a military *coup* in 1970, and embarked upon a program of modernization with the Baath Party. He adopted pan-Arabian ideas and pursued a policy of national cultural unity, which he used to dissipate tensions between the religious communities, thus stabilizing the country. He dealt harshly with all Islamist movements.

In countries such as Turkey and Egypt, nationalist movements began to embark upon programs of social and educational modernization during the 20th century, but made life difficult for the ethnic minorities within their countries such as the Kurds in Turkey and Iraq, who wanted to assert their own independence, thus inevitably provoking conflict with the central authorities. Such conflicts can be seen as the result of a frequently repressive cultural unification policy based on the idea of the nation state.

Because of the obligatory social contributions at the heart of Islam's religious and social ethics, the word "socialism" does not have any negative connotations for Muslims, whereas Marxism and Bolshevism, due to their inherent atheism, are

emphatically disapproved of. Based on earlier notions of cooperation on both economic and social planes, socialist ideas were embraced by many Islamic societies. The ideas of Egyptian president Gamal Abdel Nasser (1918–1970, state president from 1954) exerted a particularly strong attraction over the Arab world. President Nasser combined self-confidence in foreign policy with a socialist modernization program. At the same time he made himself the spokesman of "pan-Arabianism"— the idea of the "eternal Arab mission" stressing the importance of a common Arabic language and culture. One success of his pan-Arabic propaganda was the union with Syria under his leadership between 1958 and 1961. Nasser's defeat by Israel in 1967 resulted in some loss of prestige, but this did not stop many countries adopting various elements of his modernization program.

Left:
Yitzhak Rabin (1922–1995) and Yasser Arafat (1929–2004) with US president Bill Clinton

From the 1980s, a degree of understanding developed between Israel and Palestine. A handshake on the White House lawn sealed an agreement relating to Palestinian autonomy. But peace did not last and the conflict continues.

Dyer in Tunis, Tunisia

The struggle of the Maghreb countries for independence from France was long and hard. While Morocco and Tunisia became independent in 1956, the fighting in Algeria dragged on until 1962. This photograph shows the manufacture of the traditional cap that became a national symbol of the struggle for independence.

The Holy War

The skyline of Abu Dhabi in the United Arab Emirates

Muhammad expressed a number of different views on the subject of war and peace. While he called for patience during attacks by his enemies in Mecca, in Medina he emphasized the right to repel attacks by his enemies in a defensive war. His attitude toward his own offensive acts is not fully clear, although he does warn against starting unjustified wars.

The expression "holy war" is widely used in the West for *jihad*, but the Arabic term actually means a lot more than this. It shares its derivation with *ijtihad* (from *jahada*, meaning "to struggle, endeavor"), denoting the independently reasoned judgments of the *sharia*. *Jihad* therefore means committing oneself to the cause of Islam, not just going to war for it.

Jihad forms part of Islamic belief and is even frequently referred to as a "sixth pillar of Islam," but only Kharijits regard it as the personal duty of every believer. *Jihad* not only designates the fight against enemies of the faith, but also the "inner battle" for self-perfection and the fight against wrongful inclinations or the devil's powers of seduction.

Outwardly, *jihad* reveals itself as a battle against the enemies who try to turn the Muslims away from their religion. Historically this meant the Christian missionaries. Sura 2, 193 states: "Fight against them until idolatry is no more and God's religion reigns supreme." It Is therefore more a question of protecting the Islamic community than spreading the faith, as Islam traditionally knows no missionary zeal.

Islam's traditional view of the world is that it is divided into the "dar al-islam," the region (or, more accurately, "house") under Islamic rule, and the "dar al-harb," the house of war or non-Islamic world, with which treaties and agreements may be concluded. The word "harb" means war in the true military sense, but is not as a rule used in conjunction with "holy." The phrase "holy war" is more likely to derive from the ancient Israelite belief of the Hebrew Bible, which states that Yahweh (God) was the true warrior during the wars of the Israelites. The question of whether or not this idea of a belligerent God was transferred directly to Islam is a subject of dispute among scholars, and many reform-oriented scholars and jurists reject the term "holy war." Islam itself stresses that peace is the highest aim of *jihad*, and the Qur'an states that it is a Muslim's duty to be peaceful for as long as non-Muslims remain peaceful. Sura 4, 90 states: "Therefore if they keep away from you and cease their hostility and offer you peace, God bids you not to harm them." In the West *jihad* is equated with the notion of "holy war" because of parallels that have been drawn between the spread of Islam and the Christian crusades (11th–13th centuries), another disputed hypothesis.

Sultan Saladin fighting the crusaders, 1884 Illustration by Gustave Doré

The battle for Jerusalem
Painting

the course of the Iran-Iraq War (1980–1988) and under the Iraqi leader, Saddam Hussein, during the Gulf War (1991) and in the 2003 invasion of Iraq. The aggressive form of *jihad* has a particular significance for the Shiites in the context of their cult of martyrs. An individual who dies a martyr during a religious war carries the honorary Islamic title *Shahid* ("witness") and special respect is paid to his family. In addition, the Prophet declared that he will immediately be able to partake of the joys of paradise. An extremely aggressive form of *jihad* is fought by many Islamist groups in their struggle against society. Thus the Egyptian Muslim Brotherhood (during the

1920s) called for *jihad* against the supremacy of Europe over the Islamic states, and used terrorist tactics in their struggle. Despite the involvement of some Islamic groups in global and indiscriminate terrorist attacks during recent years, the concept of aggressive *jihad* meets with the approval of only a small minority of Muslims today.

The Call for *Jihad*

Historically, the Sunnites believed it was the prerogative of the caliphs, as the successors or representatives of Muhammad, to call for *jihad*. The Shiites also stress that only the legitimate successors of the Prophet, the imams, have this right. However, since the caliphate has disappeared and the 12th imam remains in hiding, many Qur'an scholars conclude that no one has the lawful right to order a war of aggression and that only defensive wars, undertaken to protect Islam, may be fought. During the course of history, there has been no shortage of calls for *jihad*, as even quarreling Muslim states have simply declared their opponents unbelievers and then gone to war. In recent times this has happened in

Muslim women, supporters of Hizbollah, at the funeral of a "martyr"
Nabatyie, Lebanon

Islamism and Fundamentalism

The term "Islamism" can be used to describe all the different groups that demand a strict and uncompromising form of Islamic rule, and the reintroduction of *sharia* law in their countries. The critical term "fundamentalism," often used synonymously in the West, is misleading as it actually refers to a Protestant movement active at the beginning of the 20th century that favored the literal truth of the Bible's account of creation over scientific explanations. Islamism is more of a political movement than a religious one, and its struggle is against the western-influenced secularization of modern society. The organizational forms and methods it employs differ greatly when considering each region in turn, ranging from the parliamentary struggle (Turkey, Jordan) via the more secret brotherhoods (Egypt,

Syria) to terrorist acts of violence (Algeria, Afghanistan). The Islamists take as their starting point the real problems facing many Islamic countries today; their demand for greater social justice wins over many supporters from the lower strata of society, and with their propaganda against the decay of values and consumerism they increasingly reach

Ayatollah Ruhollah Khomeini, (1902–1989)
Photograph taken 1978

This leading Iranian Shiite cleric had been an opponent of the lay administration of the Shah since the 1930s. As a staunch preacher against the westernization of Iran, he became the spokesman of the religious resistance and was forced to leave the country in 1964. Following his triumphant return in 1979, he was made Iran's supreme leader, despite not holding any official state office, and he called for "rule by Islamic experts." He showed increasing intolerance towards other revolutionary groups, and fought against westernization and lay society.

Afghan militiamen
Photograph taken March 1, 1988

During the Soviet occupation of Afghanistan (1979–1988), the lay regime the Soviets supported was opposed by the Islamic mujahedin. The Soviets withdrew to be replaced by military rule followed by civil war between the opposing groups, resulting in the mujahedin taking

Kabul in 1992. The radical Taliban Islamist militia won the ensuing battles among the various Islamist groups in 1994, and in 1995 conquered nearly all the cities. In 2001, the Northern Alliance and the US military won control following the September 11 attacks on the US, and by the end of 2001 an interim government was in place.

the less secure members of the middle classes and technical elite, too. However, Islamists are not reactionary conservatives, but ideologues, whose core concept is one of "opposition to the modern world" or "a modern world split in two:" whereas they oppose the aims and values of the West—for example, pluralism and freedom of worship—they not only recognize the value of its tools (such as mass media, technology, advances in medicine), but are also adept at using these themselves.

The spiritual roots of Islamism reach back to the 19th century. In the 1920s a militant form of Islamism developed in Egypt with the "Muslim Brotherhood," whose propagandist Sayyid Qutb (1906–1966) called for Muslims to fight modern "barbarism." One major theoretician was the Pakistani Abu-l-Ala al-Maudoodi (1903–1979), who wanted to replace the parliamentary

Fundamentalists in Teheran (Iran)

The Islamist movements represent an enormous challenge today for many modern Islamic states.

Anti-American demonstration on the streets of Teheran, photograph taken 1979

After the restoration in 1953 of the Shah, who fled Iran due to internal strife, he established an authoritarian regime, suppressing opposition groups. Following his overthrow in 1978, the country's anger was directed against the USA, in whose interests he had reigned.

sovereignty of the people with the "undivided sovereignty of God." The Islamist cause was given new impetus with the founding of the Ayatollah Khomeini's Islamic Republic of Iran in 1979. In general, most Islamic countries and their governments adopt a critical stance towards the Islamist struggle, or even reject it outright. Many states take steps to combat it, and the majority of Muslims feel alienated by its militancy and uncompromising views.

Islam as a Way of Life

Islam is the youngest and second largest of the world religions. Today there are nearly a billion Muslims, around one-fifth of the world's population. Islam stands for devotion to God, and choosing it as a faith must be a self-conscious act, although those with Muslim fathers are also considered Muslims themselves.

As with all major religions that spread, taking in many different peoples and cultures despite having their origins in a particular cultural region—in this case, of course, the Arab lands—Islam embraces countless different identities, branches and

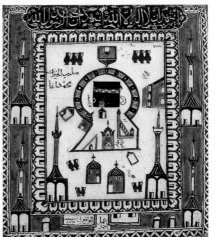

forms of usage that are all held together by the bond of a common faith in the One God, Allah and His Messenger, Muhammad. The lack of ecclesiastical structures and, thus, of a single undisputed religious authority, combined with great flexibility in adopting a wide diversity of traditions, has also contributed significantly to this pluralism.

From its very beginnings, Islam placed an emphasis on the considerable social obligations of the faith and makes community life the focal point of its blueprint for the conduct of believers' lives. Because the Prophet Muhammad was also a statesman and the political leader of his community, religion and politics are very

Below:
Ceramic tile featuring a hare
12th century
Florence, Bargello Museum

Artistic creation plays a special role in Islam. Although prohibition of the image was restricted to the religious sphere, ornament (often involving geometric, interlaced designs) became the main method used for the decoration of walls and surfaces.

Miniature of an observatory
16th century
University of Istanbul

Science has always played an important role in Islam, and the knowledge of the ancients, particularly the Greeks, was highly valued. It was adopted and further developed by all branches of science.

Religious procession
Marrakech, Morocco

In Islam, religious worship is not so much a matter of inner reflection, but more a question of practicing as part of a community. The Five Pillars of Islam in particular emphasize the greater importance of social duty over securing the private salvation of the individual. Islam's numerous religious processions and festivals also bring large numbers of believers together.

Below:
Decorative page from a Turkish Qur'an, 16th century Berlin, Museum for Islamic Art

The Qur'an is believed to be a word-for-word rendering of God's words to Muhammad and the revelation of God's laws.

King Faisal Mosque, designed by Vedat Delakoy (Turkey) in Islamabad, Pakistan 1966/86

Although God can be worshipped everywhere, the mosque has a special importance as the central house of prayer and gathering place of the community. The King Faisal Mosque combines modern architecture with traditional elements. The prayer hall holds 10,000 worshippers and the adjacent courtyard another 64,000. As is usual for major mosques, a university with its own printing press and an Institute for Islamic research are attached to it.

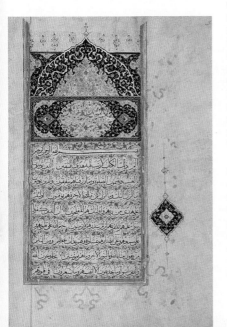

closely connected. However, there are large differences in the extent to which religious matters are allowed to influence political life. This becomes particularly relevant in the light of the belief held by many Islamic groups that the way to save modern society is through the direct implementation of their religious expectations.

The majority of Muslims recognize that Islamic communities were never ruled solely according to the religious laws, but were always influenced by the flexible approach they adopted to changing situations. In its core message, Islam is a religion of peace—as demonstrated, for example, by the close relationship between the words *islam* and *salaam* (Arabic for peace). The identity of most Muslims throughout the world is therefore characterized not only by a clear profession of faith, but also by the desire for peaceful coexistence with others in a complex world created by God.

Glossary

Abbasids
Second dynasty of caliphs 750–1258; capital: Baghdad, moved to Samarra in the ninth century. Overthrown during the Mongol invasion.

Caliph
From the Arabic *khalifa*, meaning "deputy, successor." Leaders of the Muslim community after the Prophet. Became hereditary in 661 CE and as such recognized by the Sunnis, but not by the Shiites, who rejected it as the "rule of kings." This led to an early schism.

Calligraphy
The art of fine writing and one of Islam's outstanding art forms. As Islam is a text-based religion, various forms of script developed as a way of representing religious formulae artistically and honoring God. These styles became increasingly developed and refined over time.

Fatimids
Shiite countercaliphate in Tunisia and Egypt 909–1171; capital: Mahdiya, later Cairo. Overthrown by Saladin.

Fatwa
Legal opinion requested by a believer and handed down by a jurist.

Fundamentalism
Used in the West as a synonym for Islamism. Fundamentalism was originally a Protestant

movement at the beginning of the 20th century.

Hadith
Arabic, "announcement." Collections of the Prophet Muhammad's words and deeds. In order to avoid falsification, an important aspect of a *hadith* is the "unbroken chain of those passing on the tradition" to Muhammad and his closest circle. After the Qur'an, the *hadiths* are the second most important written source of the Islamic faith.

Hajj
Ritual pilgrimage to Mecca. As one of the five basic duties (pillars) of Islam, the pilgrimage should be undertaken by every Muslim at least once during his lifetime. Those who have been on the pilgrimage carry the honorary title *hajji*.

Harem
From the Arabic *harim*, meaning "inviolable, consecrated and protected place". The women and children's living quarters, which were inaccessible to visitors. Later also the secluded and guarded women's wing of a ruler's palace.

Hijrah
The flight of Muhammad and his followers from Mecca to Medina in 622 CE. Also marks the beginning of the Islamic calendar.

Ijtihad
From the Arabic meaning "to struggle on one's own."

The independently reasoned legal decision of a jurist based on his study of the sources and application of his own reason. Largely abandoned by the Sunni community following the establishment of the schools of law in the 11th–12th centuries, the Shiites continued to adhere to it. The term is today interpreted differently by the various law schools as a result of attempts to adapt the Islamic legal system to modernization initiatives and changing circumstances.

Imam
True meaning, "model, leader." For today's Sunnis, a community's prayer leader; for the Shiites, the physical descendant of Muhammad or Ali and leader of the Islamic community at large. The various Shiite groups recognize different numbers of imams.

Imamites
Twelver Shiites. The largest Shiite group; since 1501 the official state religion of Iran. Belief in the return of the "imam in hiding" at the end of time.

Islamism
Collective term for the "anti-modern" ideologies of political groups who fight against modernization and secularization, and believe in an uncompromising form of Islam as the only valid authority in society as well as restoration of the Islamic

legal system, the *sharia*. Various different methods are used in the struggle, ranging from propaganda to terrorist attack.

Ismailis
Sevener Shiites. The least united and most complex of the Shiite groups, they are characterized by speculative systems of thought often combined with socio-revolutionary tendencies. They continue to exist in various subgroups today.

Jihad
From the Arabic *jahada*, meaning "to struggle." Often inaccurately translated as "holy war." Jihad denotes the personal contribution every Muslim is expected to make to the spread of Islam and to establishing the order on earth desired by God. This goes far beyond engaging in battle. Today, the meaning of the term is restricted by Islamist groups to the armed struggle for strict Islamic rule.

Ka'bah
Cube-shaped main holy shrine of the Muslims in the Great Mosque of Mecca. The building houses the black stone and, according to tradition, was built by Abraham in honor of the One God.

Kharijites
"The seceders." Strict early-Islam orientation; first Islamic group to split away

(657). The Khajirites only recognize the first two Rightly Guided Caliphs and formed their own states.

Laicism
Concept that originated in France in the 19th century, representing an anti-clerical attitude that strives for the separation of Church and state.

Madrasa
Islamic school or university where theology and jurisprudence are taught, usually attached to a mosque complex. Established as a form of educational institution by the Seljuks in the 11th century.

Mahdi
Arabic, "the rightly guided one." First used as an epithet of respect, for example for Abraham of Muhammad, the figure of the Mahdi plays an important role primarily for Shiite groups, who await the return of the Mahdi (the imam in hiding) as the redeemer at the end of time. Historically, various different Muslim leaders have claimed either to be the Mahdi or to be charged with preparing for his coming.

Mihrab
Prayer niche for the prayer leader set into the *qibla* wall of the mosque. It usually takes the form of a semicircular recess with a pillar at each side of its opening.

Minaret
Tower from which the muezzin calls the faithful to prayer. Originally a high tower next to the mosque (later also two or four towers incorporated into the mosque complex), the minaret is an important component of the Friday mosque.

Minbar
Pulpit from which the preacher delivers the Friday sermon. Usually made of wood and in the early period moveable, today normally positioned next to the *mihrab*.

Muezzin
Caller to prayer, who summons the faithful to prayer five times a day from the minaret.

Mutazilites
Adherents of a rationalist strand of Islamic theology and philosophy, who believed that the Qur'an was "created." In the ninth century they were responsible for the official state teaching in the caliphate.

Ornament
Artistic wall and surface decoration that plays an important role in all areas of Islamic art and architecture, due to the prohibition of representational images. Its most widespread form was characterized by geometric patterns and interlacing vegetal motifs.

Qadi
Judge responsible for, among other things, the guardianship of certain individuals, attestations and the supervision of religious foundations.

Qibla
Direction of prayer towards Mecca, which the Prophet established in 624 CE. Each mosque has a *qibla* wall to which the faithful turn for prayer.

Qur'an
From the Arabic *al-quran*, meaning "reading, lecture." Islam's holy book, which contains the revelations of the Prophet Muhammad, believed to be the direct, word-for-word message of God to mankind.

Rightly Guided Caliphs
According to the Sunnah branch of Islam, the first four caliphs (community leaders) after the death of Muhammad. They were not hereditary, but were close companions of the Prophet, which is a fundamental difference between Sunni and Shiite Muslims.

Sharia
The Islamic legal system, regarded as an essential element of Muslim belief and a central component of the Islamic community. As Islam is a lay religion and does not have any comprehensive theology, the Qur'an scholars act primarily as teachers of jurisprudence and provide believers with practical, everyday help. The *sharia* is considered the guarantor of the divine order on earth.

Shia/Shiites
From the Arabic *shiat Ali*, meaning "the part of Ali." Minority of Muslims (around 10 percent) who regard Ali and his successors as the sole legitimate leaders of the Muslim community and reject the rule of the caliphs. Split into different groups, most of them believe in the return of the Mahdi or imam in hiding at the end of time.

Sunna/Sunnis
Arabic, meaning "usage, custom." The totality of the practices—that is, words and deeds of the Prophet Muhammad and his companions as described in the *hadiths*. The Sunnis named after them today represent the majority of Muslims (around 90 percent) and recognize the caliphs as Muhammad's legitimate successors.

Sura
Chapter or section of the Qur'an. The Qur'an consists of 114 suras of decreasing length, each of them named after a particular theme.

Umayyads
First dynasty of caliphs, 661–750 CE. Capital: Damascus. A branch of the dynasty ruled as the emirs and caliphs of Córdoba, 756–1031.

Ummah
The Islamic community in its totality.

Zaydis
Fiver Shiites. The most tolerant of the Shiite groups, they are united in their belief that the legitimate line of imams ends with Zayd, the son of the fourth imam. They reject the wider Shiite belief in the return of the lost imam.

Index

CE **(Common Era)** and BCE **(Before Common Era)** are culturally and religiously neutral terms. The era to which they refer is exactly the same as the Gregorian (Solar) calendar. Therefore 1 CE = AD 1 and 1 BCE = 1 BC.

Calendar

The Islamic calendar, which is still in use today, began with the flight of the Prophet from Mecca to Medina. It is based on the lunar year, lasting 12 months. As the lunar year is roughly 11 days shorter than the solar year, the beginning of the Islamic year only coincides with the beginning of the solar year every 33 years.

Cover
Taj Mahal in Agra (India),
1632–1643
Photo © Thomas Dix,
Grenzach-Wyhlen

Illustration p. 2
Ka'bah **at night**
Camerapix, Nairobi
(photograph:
Mohamed Amin)

Back cover
Sura 27 "The Ant",
Verses 36–39
North Africa, 12th century
Qur'an manuscript in
Maghribi-Duktus, Spike
College, London
Photo © AKG, Berlin

Impressum

© 2006 Tandem Verlag GmbH
KÖNEMANN is a trademark and an imprint of Tandem Verlag GmbH

Editor: Peter Delius
Series concept: Ludwig Könemann
Art Director: Peter Feierabend
Concept, editorial and layout: Susanne Brown
Picture research: Katleen Krause
Cover: Malzkorn Kommunikation & Gestaltung, Köln

Original title: *Minireligionsführer Islam*
ISBN-10: 3-8331-2521-7 (of the original German edition)
ISBN-13: 978-3-8331-2521-8 (of the original German edition)

© 2006 for the English edition: Tandem Verlag GmbH
KÖNEMANN is a trademark and an imprint of Tandem Verlag GmbH

Translation from German: Richard Elliott in association with
Cambridge Publishing Management
Copy-editor: Sandra Stafford in association with
Cambridge Publishing Management
Updater: Jenni Rainford in association with Cambridge
Publishing Management
Typesetting: Cambridge Publishing Management
Project management: Gabriela Hallas and Jackie Dobbyne
for Cambridge Publishing Management

Printed in China

ISBN-10: 3-8331-2524-1
ISBN-13: 978-3-8331-2524-9

10 9 8 7 6 5 4 3 2 1
X IX VIII VII VI V IV III II I

Issues in the Intelligence Debate

Issues in the Intelligence Debate

A juxtaposition of the arguments
and an appraisal
by Professor Denis H. Stott of
Intelligence: The Battle for the Mind
by H. J. Eysenck and L. J. Kamin

NFER-Nelson

Published by The NFER-Nelson Publishing Company Ltd.,
Darville House, 2 Oxford Road East,
Windsor, Berks. SL4 1DF.

First published 1983
© Denis H. Stott, 1983
ISBN 0-7005-0553-9
Code 8140 02 1

Photoset in Baskerville by Illustrated Arts
Printed in Great Britain by
The Whitefriars Press Ltd., Tonbridge

Distributed in the USA by Humanities Press Inc.,
Atlantic Highlands, New Jersey 07716 USA

Contents

Introduction

This booklet originated in my own difficulty, during the reading of the Eysenck and Kamin debate on intelligence, in matching evidence and counter-evidence, accusation and counter-accusation. I decided that, with my limited resources of memory, the only way I could reach a judicious appraisal was to place evidence and rejoinder in juxtaposition. In the course of this exercise I came to appreciate the similar problems that not only the general reader but also the professional psychologist would have in weighing up the conflicting evidence and claims. There is a danger that their confusion may engender in them a mood of impatience with what must be reckoned one of the outstanding psychological and educational questions of our century. It occurred to me that my rearrangement of the evidence and arguments might serve as a sort of summing up before a jury. At least it should bring the points in dispute into sharper focus.

In the main I have left the reader to form his own judgments. Where I felt it necessary to verify sources, I report what I found. Occasionally, also, I dipped into my own files for further evidence which had a bearing on the issues raised by either Eysenck or Jensen, but I refrained from developing at length any new argument or producing evidence on issues not already raised in the debate.

The subject of the debate

To remind the reader what the issue is, Eysenck is defending his position that approximately 80 per cent of the variability in individual 'intelligence', as fairly accurately reflected in IQ test scores, is due to genetic factors, this meaning that these are on the whole twice as important as the environmental determinants (pp. 160–1). Kamin does not formally deny that there is any genetic element in IQ scores (he does not apparently subscribe to the concept of 'intelligence'), but rather disregards it. The thrust of his attack on the Eysenck position is that the experimental findings might feasibly be explained solely in terms of environmental differences.

My original tabular juxtaposition became too cumbersome to reproduce in its original form, so I have taken each of the issues in turn and juxtaposed the evidence and arguments in a continuous text. Since the structure of the debate was that Eysenck advanced his thesis and Kamin attacked it, I have, under each topic, summarized Eysenck's evidence and argument first, and followed it by Kamin's rejoinders.

Eysenck in general refrains from dealing in detail with Kamin's criticisms of the twin, adoption and other studies upon which he bases his estimate of the role played by genetic factors, referring the reader to the review of Kamin's 1974 book by David Fulker in the *American Journal of Psychology* (1975). This review, according to Eysenck, shows that 'Kamin has fallen into errors at least as grievous as those made by the psychologists he criticises' (p. 158). A few pages later (p. 164), he goes even further, claiming that 'Fulker, in his review of Kamin's book, lists many almost incredible statistical errors'. Eysenck does not reproduce Fulker's criticisms, although they were made in a journal not easily available to British readers of the debate. My juxtaposition of the arguments would thus be one-sided if I did not summarize Fulker's arguments. Since their inclusion in the main text would risk overburdening it with technicalities they figure at the end of each section. Moreover, their technical character renders inappropriate the method I have used in the main text, that of placing the arguments side by side and letting the reader judge with a minimum of comment on my part. I have consequently attempted a limited evaluation of them, asking myself two questions. The first is, does Fulker establish, as Eysenck claims, that Kamin has made 'almost incredible statistical errors'? The second is whether Fulker succeeds in substantially destroying the value of Kamin's arguments against the hereditarian case.

My own biases

The first query that will arise in the reader's mind is my personal stance in this controversy. Essentially it has been that the interaction between heredity and environment is so continuous, intricate, variable, cumulative and specific that no general statement can be made about their relative contributions. The modern view of the nature of genetic programming is that it conditions the cells of the body to respond in a certain way to each environmental contingency.

(Dobzhansky 1973, 1962; Caspari 1977; Denenberg 1977). If I may presume to quote my earlier statement: 'To ask whether given individual variations are more due to the variability of the genetic instructions or to that of the environment is not to ask one question, but a thousand or a hundred thousand – according to where we stop following the alternatives.' (Stott 1960). In short, I hold the view that the simple additive model of genetic and environmental 'contributions' bears no relation to reality.

Lest I be dubbed an environmentalist let me state that I stand on what would by current fashion be judged the genetic wing of opinion as far as the determination of behaviour is concerned. From my study of the effectiveness-behaviour of a young child (Stott 1961) I argued, against the weight of the child-development theory of the time, that the desires to explore and to recognize, to create notable effects and to achieve objectives could not originate in social conditioning but were instinctive, i.e. genetically conditioned ways of dealing with the environment. I have brought forward evidence which suggests the existence of genetic provisions for limiting as well as increasing competence (Stott 1962). And I see hundreds of petty human actions and likes and dislikes as genetic programming for dealing with specific environmental contingencies.

If I were asked to say which class of genetically originating instinctive tendencies were most responsible for individual differences in mental functioning I would name those of intrinsic motivation. These I see as conditioning the breadth and depth and organization of the individual's experiences, and their consolidation into concepts and skills. In the words of a little known philosopher (Overstreet 1926), 'The mind becomes what it does.' The concept of an independent structure of 'intelligence' which can be inherited as such is quite foreign to this developmental view of mental capabilities.

On the subject of environmental influences, I perceive the most important of these as arising from cultural differences of an ingrained and persistent character, only very imperfectly measured by socioeconomic status but reflected in social-class and ethnic differences. I see these cultural differences as combining with variations of individual motivation to produce a diversity of learning skills which, acting from earliest childhood, are the principal regulators of the individual's mental development (Stott 1978). It is in such terms that I prefer to think of an interaction of heredity and environment resulting in a wide range of intellectual capabilities. (I also prefer not to use the word 'intelligence'.)

Lastly, I would fault both protagonists in this dispute for their neglect of the intrauterine environment. I feel that I have good empirical grounds for believing that it is during the period of gestation –

when cell division occurs at the fastest rate – that the most important genetic-environmental interactions occur, conditioning the child's subsequent pattern of motivation and behaviour and hence the development of his mental skills (Stott 1973, 1976). It would nevertheless be outside the scope of this book to deal with this issue at length.

In the remainder of this book each of the issues raised in the debate between Eysenck and Kamin is dealt with in turn. The page references given in brackets refer to the volume in which the debate was published, *Intelligence: The Battle for the Mind* (Eysenck and Kamin 1981) unless it is evident from the context that they apply to another work.

Identical twins reared apart

Eysenck (p. 49) bases his case on 'three major studies' but does not name them except for specifically excluding Burt's. In his 1979 book (p. 109), however, he names – in addition to Burt's – those of Newman and colleagues (1937), Shields (1962) and Juel-Nielsen (1965), so we may assume that he is referring to the latter three. From these he notes that genetic factors account for about 77 per cent of IQ variability, but he is prepared to reduce this by 9 per cent to allow for the non-randomness of the environments of the separated twins, thus achieving agreement with the figure of 68 per cent arrived at by Erlenmeyer-Kimling and Jarvik (1963). He does not say how he arrives at this 9 per cent, and this must be borne in mind when he claims (p. 47) for quantitative estimates of heritability that *'regardless of the method used, they arrive at pretty similar values'* (Eysenck's italics). He then raises the genetic contribution to about 80 per cent to allow for the chance factors which tend to lower correlations. In doing so he assumes that in the twin studies the chance factors operated impartially to blur the genetic effects, although he has already conceded that the similarity of the environments of the separated twins could have accounted for 9 per cent of the variability. Since a large part of the debate centres around the possibility that other factors – imperfect test-standardization for age, incompleteness of separation, tester-bias, bias in selection of the sample, and so on – may also have raised the correlations, this assumption that the methodological imperfections of the twin-studies would *lower* them may be regarded as begging the question.

Eysenck bases his case for a substantial heritability of IQ on this consensus of findings of the various twin and other studies, which he regards as overriding their methodological imperfections. Consequently he undertakes no defence of the studies of separated identi-

cal (MZ) twins, despite the criticisms to which they have been subjected, and devotes less than half a page to them (p. 49).

Kamin, on the other hand, subjects each of the three studies of
separated twins to close scrutiny. In the Newman study (pp. 111–2)
he points out that twins who described themselves as differing in dis-
position were excluded on the suspicion that they were not MZ. He
also casts doubt on the method of selection, which was by invitation
through newspaper advertisement and the offer of a free trip to
Chicago. He quotes evidence which suggests that at least two of the 19
pairs pretended they were separated but were not. Thirdly, the 1916
version of the Stanford-Binet test used in the Newman study shows a
negative correlation with age, and the standardization contained no
women. Most of the Newman twins were women. Kamin points out
that if people of the same age and sex, as identical twins necessarily
are, tend to get similar test scores, the correlation would be inflated.
Eysenck does not answer this point.

In the Shields study (pp. 107–9) Kamin draws attention to the
extraordinarily large age-range of the twins (eight to 59 years) with
the same possibility of a distorted correlation. Shields, unlike Burt,
made his data available, so that Kamin was able to break down the
correlation of the twins' IQs according to whom the separated twin
was placed with. Of the 40 twin-pairs, 27 were reared in related
branches of the same biological family; for these the IQ correlation
was 0.83. For the 13 pairs reared in unrelated families it was only 0.51.
Moreover, among the 24 pairs of whom one was raised by the mother

there were 12 where the other twin was placed with one of her relatives; their IQ correlation was 0.94. That of the 12 pairs placed
elsewhere was 0.56. Kamin adduces the above differences as evidence
of the effects of similar environment.

Kamin further doubts whether many of the Shields twins experienced much separation, since the criterion for their inclusion in the
study was no more than that they had been reared in different homes
for five years of their childhoods. Some had not been separated until
the ages of 7, 8 or 9, and Kamin quotes Shield's admission of continued contact in some cases even during the separation.

The third of Kamin's criticisms of the Shields study relates to
unconscious tester-bias. He calculates that the IQ correlation for the
33 twins tested by Shields himself was 0.84; that for the five tested by
different examiners was a mere 0.11.

Fourthly, Kamin claimed that Shields did not use well standardized tests which could not be satisfactorily converted into orthodox
IQs. This is the only one of Kamin's criticisms of the separated-twins
studies that Eysenck answers in detail (p. 165). He points out that the
Dominoes test – one of those used by Shields – was very widely used in

the British Army during the war and was 'standardized on a larger and more random sample of the population than most other tests in existence'.

He does not specifically claim that the Dominoes test was adequately standardized for women (the Shields twins were again predominantly females) and over an age range from eight to 59 years. Eysenck makes the same claim for Raven's Mill Hill vocabulary test. However, Shields used only part of the latter, and doubled the scores to equalize their weighting with the Dominoes test, thus giving some 55 per cent of the variance to verbal items. Kamin's claim that Shields did not use well standardized tests is an arguable one, but in any case of little importance beside his other criticisms of the Shields twin study.

In the third of the studies of separated twins, that by Juel-Nielsen in Denmark, Kamin (p. 113) is able to show that the faulty age-standardization of the Raven Matrices Test actually resulted in a negative correlation of 0.65 between the twins' ages and the test-scores. Since each twin-pair were necessarily of the same age, this would substantially inflate the IQ correlation. Juel-Nielsen's criterion for separation was apparently also a very lenient one. Kamin quotes the case of one of the 12 pairs who lived with their own mother between the ages of seven and 14 years, and associated closely together, attended the same school and dressed alike even during the period of separation.

The data of the three above twin studies, unlike that of Burt, were fully and meticulously documented. Just as Kamin was able to draw on them for his critique, so they are available as the basis of an equally factual rebuttal on the part of Eysenck. Unfortunately in the debate he did not do this, referring the reader to Fulker's review of Kamin's 1974 book (p. 158). The latter does indeed contain a series of careful criticisms of Kamin's arguments on the twin and other studies; these are now discussed.

Fulker's criticism of Kamin (identical twins reared apart)

The first issue upon which Fulker challenges Kamin is that of the effect of the twins' widely varying ages on the correlations of their IQs. Kamin (1974) makes bold to claim, with regard to the Newman study, that, 'The correlation between the twins' IQs may be entirely due to their identical ages, rather than to their identical genes'. His argument is based on the poor standardization of the Stanford Binet test and its inadequate allowance for age – such that, as used by Newman et al. – the highest possible IQ for an individual of 16 years or older was 122. The older the testees the worse they did on the test. It follows that, since each twin-pair was of identical age, the bias of the test against older persons would affect each twin equally, and thus tend to make them more similar in IQ. The 19 pairs in the Newman study varied in age from 8 to 59 years, so that there was plenty of scope for this age bias to operate. Nevertheless, the overall correlation with age in this study was only −0.22. If this had been due to an evenly operating tendency, it would, according to Fulker, have accounted for only some 4 per cent of the IQ variation, and have reduced the twin-pair correlation only marginally from 0.67 to 0.65. Kamin maintains that the effect was not an even one, and so the correlation between IQ and age cannot be written off in this way. Fulker accepts this as reasonable, but finds it hard to believe that it was so uneven (non-linear) as almost completely to determine the resemblance of the twins in IQ. Kamin's point is that an overall age/IQ correlation of zero could hide an age-effect: at some age-bands the test could depress the scores, at others enhance them, and the only way to avoid this is to have perfect standardization of the test for all ages. Kamin admits the difficulty of estimating age/IQ correlation appropriately in a small sample of 19 with widely varying ages; and indeed the separate correlations for each sex present a confusing picture (−0.78 for the 14 males but only −0.11 for the 24 females). While admitting that the procedure is absurd because of the small numbers, Kamin breaks up the female twin-pairs into three age-groups, and gets much higher age/IQ correlations. For the two youngest pairs it comes to 0.99, but only because, as Fulker points out, both the twins of one pair had higher IQs than the other pair and were also older.

It should be emphasized that in this argument Fulker nowhere accuses Kamin of statistical error. Both agree that there is no accepted statistical technique for resolving the issue. And while Kamin makes one interpretation of this indeterminate position, namely that the age-biases of the test could have accounted for the whole of the twin-pair correlation for IQ, Fulker, from his equally committed viewpoint, refuses to agree that the age-bias could make much difference.

Kamin then demonstrated the effect of age-bias by an ingenious 'pseudopairing procedure'. He arranged the twin-pairs in order of age, and switched the IQs of adjacent pairs. This had the effect of removing any genetic effect, but since the adjacent pairs were near to each other in age, an age-bias, albeit somewhat less than in the original sample, would remain. For the seven male pairs the true correlation was 0.58; the pseudopairing gave one of 0.67. When the three female pairs of equivalent age were added, the true correlation rose to 0.65 compared with a pseudocorrelation of 0.47. For the seven elderly female pairs, however, the true correlation is 0.48 but the pseudo only 0.06. Kamin accepts from this that 'not all of the IQ correlation between twins can be attributed to age' but that this does not mean that they have to be attributed to genetic effects (Kamin also adduces similarity of environment). His final conclusion was that the 0.67 correlation between the IQs of the Newman twin-pairs 'was to some considerable extent inflated by age-bias'. He did not, as imputed to him by Fulker, claim that the age effect 'almost completely determines the resemblance of twins in IQ' (p. 506).

Fulker accepts Kamin's pseudopairing technique as 'perfectly valid', but shows that he obtained the striking age-effect by the manner in which he applied it to sections of the sample. When Fulker applied it to the whole sample, the pseudocorrelation came to only 0.12 compared with the true correlation of 0.65. My own feeling is that the pseudopairings of the twins' IQs applied to sections was too contrived to be convincing as a demonstration of a massive age effect. Nevertheless there was some age effect which must have raised the correlations of the identical twins' IQs. However, Kamin made no 'almost incredible statistical error' in the pseudopairing procedure.

In the Juel-Nielsen study of 12 separated twin-pairs Kamin found (true) age/IQ correlations of 0.61 for the 18 females and a negative 0.82 for the six males. Fulker regards this as a demonstration of 'the bizarre statistical properties of small samples'. He finds it incredible that faulty test standardization could work heavily one way for males and heavily the other way for females. Kamin finds a pseudocorrelation for the females of 0.59, which exactly equals the true correlation; and Fulker, pooling the sexes, finds one of –0.12, suggesting that the age-factor somewhat detracted from the true correlation. One reason for this confused state of affairs may well have been the advanced ages of the Juel-Nielsen twins: the average age of the women was 52.6, the oldest being 72 years; that of the males was 48, the eldest being 77! Perhaps elderly ladies do respond differently to IQ tests compared with elderly men.

One is left with the impression that both the Newman and the Juel-Nielsen samples were so small and ill-assorted that bizarre results could be expected. Probably more important than the awarding of points to the two contestants is a general conclusion that these two studies contained too many elements of unreliability to serve for the calculation of the heritability of 'intelligence' within the human race.

Fulker agrees that the studies of separated twins contain flaws in the form of severe testing bias and what he terms selective placement, but queries Kamin's claim that these are so extreme as to invalidate the studies completely.

In the matter of tester-bias Kamin adduces a telling statistic in the Shields study. For the 35 twin-pairs tested by Shields himself, the mean IQ difference was 8.5; for the five pairs of whom one or both were tested by another tester it was 22.4. Fulker tries to minimize the import of the latter figure by pointing out that in one pair neither was tested by Shields and in another the IQ difference was only 10 points, which was no more than for some of the twins wholly tested by Shields. Thus, argues Fulker, the imputation of tester-bias rests on only three cases. These considerations are irrelevant to the issue. The point was that in five cases, assuming Shields did not know in advance the results obtained by the other testers, he could not have been influenced by them; bias was ruled out, however close in IQ a pair might be, or whether Shields tested one or neither of a pair. On the other hand bias was possible in the 35 pairs tested entirely by Shields himself. Kamin's suggestion of bias is founded on the much greater differences between the mean IQ of the first group compared with that of the second.

Fulker then sought reasons for the highly divergent scores of the three pairs that remained after his exclusion of the above two. One twin failed to understand the instructions for the Dominoes test, and was excluded by Shields on that account. Kamin, however, points out (p. 110) that Shields later had them tested on the Wechsler and found them to have a difference of 19 IQ points, one of the largest recorded for separated MZ twins. Another pair had extremely divergent neuroticism scores. If this were held to invalidate IQ scores there would be very few individuals left in the subnormal range: in a survey of British educationally subnormal school children (Stott 1961) some 45 per cent evidenced unforthcomingness, the rough equivalent of neuroticism on the Bristol Social Adjustment Guides. In addition, one twin in this neurotically discrepant pair had a medical history of recurrent blindness, congenital syphilis and amnesia. But Kamin (p. 110) points out that it was this twin who had by far the higher IQ. The remaining pair were placed in extremely diverse environments. Kamin retorts that if this was the reason for the wide discrepancy in their IQs, surely this is an argument for a substantial environmental influence.

In sum, by his attempt to whittle down the number not tested exclusively by Shields, Fulker failed to detroy Kamin's imputation of tester-bias in the Shields study. Of course, with the small numbers involved, Kamin was not able to demonstrate bias conclusively. There is, on the other hand, a growing realization among psychologists that tester-bias is to be expected unless stringent precautions are taken against it. For example, Blatt and Garfunkel (1969), in their evaluation of the Skodak-Skeels follow-up studies showing large increases in IQ of children in an enriched environment, take the position that, 'unless one were sure that appropriate measures were taken to control for bias on the part of those administering the psychological tests, it is not unreasonable to contend that tester-bias may have selectively contributed to the findings'. They list among such precautions that of 'obtaining examiners who are truly ignorant of the purposes of the study' (p. 22). None of the studies of separated MZ twins incorporated such precautions, so that, because of the expectation that identical twins would be very similar in IQ, the results were likely to contain a systematic but unknown amount of bias in favour of the genetic hypothesis.

Lastly on the subject of separated twins, Fulker in the main accepts Kamin's criticism of the Burt study, but considers that Burt 'has probably been guilty more of a careless reporting that stemmed from a disregard for sample size . . . than of any attempt to mislead' (p. 511). Two paragraphs later Fulker criticises Kamin's (1974) 'tendency to obsessively overemphasize idiosyncratic detail'. If more of us had adopted Kamin's methods of scrutiny, Burt's work would have been exposed as fraudulent long ago.

IQ resemblance of MZ and DZ twins and non-twin siblings

Eysenck's argument is that, if 'intelligence' is largely hereditary, monozygotic twins should show a much greater resemblance in IQ scores than dizygotic twins. He quotes but one study, (Herrman and Hogben in 1932) which supports this hypothesis in that the mean IQ difference for the MZ twins was 9.2 compared with 17.7 for DZ twins of the same sex, 17.9 for DZ twins of opposite sex, and 16.8 for non-twin siblings (pp. 47–8). Eysenck further draws attention to the overall similarity of the means of DZs of each sex to each other, and to the means for siblings. This is what a genetic explanation of IQ differences would predict. 'These results,' he assures us, 'are typical of much later work, and they are quite clear-cut.' (p. 48). He does not quote the later work in the debate, but in his 1979 book (p. 108) refers the reader to the 14 studies listed in the Erlenmeyer–Kimling and Jarvik (1963) table.

The finding of the Herrman–Hogben study that DZ twins are no more alike than ordinary siblings is interpreted by Eysenck as indicating 'that twins are not treated differently from ordinary brothers and sisters in any ways that affect intelligence' (p. 48). He further refers to the study by Loehlin and Nichols (1976) as showing that the ways in which twins were treated 'had absolutely no effect' on their intellectual ability.

Kamin (p. 128) challenges Eysenck's argument from three angles. First he quotes Nichols (1965) as showing that female DZs tend to report more similar experiences than male DZs, which on an environmentalist hypothesis should result in higher IQ correlations for female DZs. Kamin (1979) draws on 13 twin studies in which IQs were given by sexes. In ten the female DZs did indeed resemble each other significantly more than did the male DZs (p. 128). Among these was a study by Huntley (1966) in which the inter-twin correlation for 86 male DZ pairs was 0.51 and that for the female DZs 0.70, the latter being not significantly lower than that for the female MZs. Kamin shows that this surprising result could not have been due to the misclassification of some DZs as MZ, since the same classification showed no such pattern in the correlations for height.

Second, Kamin quotes two studies (p. 132) in which the IQ correlations for DZ pairs were significantly higher than those for ordinary siblings. In that by Herrman and Hogben, the very one that Eysenck quotes, the correlation for the DZs is 0.49 but for the siblings only 0.32. That by Tabah and Sutter produced correlations of 0.58 and 0.45 respectively. Kamin is aware that the different ages of the siblings would lower their IQ correlation relatively to that of the twinpairs, who were of course of the same age, but he discovered a study (p. 132) (by Record, McKeown and Edwards 1969), in which both twins and the siblings were tested at exactly the same age. The correlation for the 358 opposite-sex twin pairs was 0.62, compared with 0.55 for the 2,525 pairs of opposite-sex siblings. Kamin argues that these results do indicate a greater similarity of environment for DZ twins than for ordinary siblings in a way that affects their IQs.

Third, Kamin quotes studies which seem to suggest that differences of treatment affect IQ. Reanalysing the raw data of that by Loehlin and Nichols (fortunately available on computer tape) which Eysenck had quoted as evidence that treatment made no difference, Kamin calculated that MZ twins whose parents had tried to treat them exactly alike were significantly more alike in IQ than the MZ twins whose parents had not done so.

Reanalysing Scarr's (1980) raw data, Kamin found that the MZ pairs who said that they *almost always* dressed alike differed in IQ by an average of 5.7 IQ points on the Raven Matrices, while those who *seldom* dressed alike differed by 10.7 points, this difference being statistically significant (pp. 130–1). (Scarr had reported no difference, but she amalgamated a four point graduated scale of answers into a simple Yes or No about dressing alike). Eysenck retorts (p. 164) that it is 'preposterous' to suggest that such factors as dressing alike can have any real effect on intelligence and that Kamin's argument 'does not stand up to examination for one minute'. But he does not demonstrate any fault in Kamin's statistics, telling us merely that Kamin 'eschews proper statistical evaluation of the data'. In effect Kamin had never suggested that dressing alike as such could influence intelligence; he characterized it as a very insensitive measure of similarity of treatment, but one which nevertheless produced a significant difference (p. 131).

Kamin admits that the IQ differences resulting from differences in treatment were not great. The most he achieves is to undermine the assumption that the greater IQ resemblance of MZ over DZ twins can be treated as a measure of genetic influence which is exact enough to serve as a basis for a calculation of heritability (p. 109).

Fulker's criticism of Kamin (twin/sibling and DZ-twin/twin comparisons)

Kamin takes as a critical test of the genetic hypothesis a comparison of the correlations between, firstly, DZ twin-pairs and, secondly, one member of a DZ pair and a sibling. He argues that if IQ is largely genetically determined, both correlations should be similar, because DZ twins are no more alike genetically than they are to their siblings. If, on the other hand, IQ is largely environmentally determined, and twins share with each other a much more similar environment than they do with their non-twin sibs, the correlations for the DZ twins should be much higher than those between one twin and a sibling. He could find only four studies in which this comparison was made. In three of them the DZ correlations were markedly higher than the twin/sib correlations. Fulker calculates the same correlations from a study by Reed and Reed (1965) and gets substantially the same result. All five comparisons are given in Table 1 (page 51).

From an examination of the raw data for the Reed and Reed study Fulker suggests three reasons for the low correlations of the sibling twin-pairs. First, he found that the variance for the twins was lower than that for sibs, and using the sib variance in the denominator to calculate the sib/twin correlation raises it from 0.34 to 0.37. He regards this as not strikingly lower than the 0.45 for the sib/sib correlation. Nevertheless it remains much lower than the 0.60 for the DZ twins. Second, he found that when the eleven most discrepant of the 71 twin/sib pairs were removed, the difference between them and the sib/sib group largely disappeared. Fulker does not show that these eleven pairs or their families were by any independent criterion a special subgroup, and there seems no reason for their removal except to manipulate the correlations. One is tempted to wonder what he would have said if Kamin had made a similar manipulation.

Fulker further observed that in the families of ten of the eleven most discrepant twin-sib pairs the mean IQ for the twins was lower than that for the sib pairs, which suggests that the high DZ correlation was due to a 'variable deficit between families', i.e. a tendency for both of a pair of DZ twins to be impaired if one is impaired. In nearly all studies the mean IQ of twins is lower than that for non-twin siblings, which suggests congenital damage. Since the reasons for the manifestation of the handicaps in question cannot be genetic or they would not appear specifically in twins, they must be due to the intrauterine environment or the birth process – another environmental difference between twins and non-twins which neither Fulker nor Kamin took into account.

Fulker's third point relates to Kamin's reason for the high twin/twin and the low twin/sib correlations relative to those for sib/sibs, this being that twins create for themselves a special environment and are consequently less close to their non-twin sibs than ordinary sibs would be to each other. Fulker found that after the removal of the eleven families containing the discrepant twin/sib pairs, the twin/twin correlation remained largely unchanged (actually rising to 0.61 from 0.60). Hence, he argued, the greater IQ resemblance of DZ twins could not be an effect of their greater closeness relative to their other siblings. It would, however, be surprising if the mere closeness of twins to each other and their distance from their non-twin siblings would alone produce a massive difference in their mental development. The shared environment of twins goes further than their relations with each other and their other siblings. It includes a shared prenatal environment, which means sharing the hormones, nutrition and oxygen supply of mothers subjected to the same physical illnesses and emotional stresses.

Kamin observed that male DZ twins, in three studies, were more dissimilar in their IQs than female DZs (1974, p. 99). He attributed this to the greater closeness of girl twins to each other than male twins. Fulker (p. 516) scrutinizes the F ratios, as measures of the significance of differences in the variances for each sex, and queries one of them. On the other hand, for the Clark–Vandenberg–Proctor study he selects the lowest (non-significant) F ratio of 1.41 for Raven's Progressive Matrices, but ignores that of 3.25 for the PMA verbal test. This could have been an oversight. Fulker then quotes three additional studies (p. 517) in which the greater variability of male DZ twins did not obtain. There is thus no impressive evidence for such a sex difference, and it is doubtful whether, when found, it can be attributed to the greater closeness of female twins. It could also arise from the greater liability to congenital damage of males, which would be more pronounced in twins as a high-risk group. The consequent greater mortality among male twins could also account for the much smaller number of male than of female DZ twins found in school samples, which Kamin adduces as additional evidence that male DZ twins experience more dissimilar environments.

Types of environmental effect in twin studies

Eysenck (p. 161) accuses Kamin of mixing up within-family and between-family differences in twin studies which, he claims, 'are two quite different factors'. 'This', he goes on to say, 'is a very important point: sometimes he (Kamin) argues as if the contribution were entirely of one kind, and at other times as if it were entirely of the other kind'. Thus, in dealing with separated MZ twins, Kamin is accused of 'neglecting the fact that their within-family environments were entirely different'. Kamin did not neglect this 'fact': on the contrary he showed that a great many of the twins were brought up in rather similar within-family environments. That there was a much greater IQ similarity in those twins reared by maternal relatives than in those reared by paternal relatives strongly suggests a cultural similarity in method of upbringing. It is consequently very unlikely that 'the within-family environments were entirely different' for separated MZ twins. Kamin did not stress the distinction between internal and external environmental indices, and indeed there was no point in doing so: cultural influences operate both 'within-family' and between-family'.

When it comes to differences between MZ and DZ twins, Eysenck accuses Kamin of being 'entirely concerned with slight discrepancies in upbringing' (within-family) and of disregarding 'the absence of between-family environmental variance'. It is true that, in seeking an environmental explanation for MZ/DZ differences and the greater IQ similarity of DZs compared with ordinary siblings, Kamin does concentrate on what must mostly be within-family differences, i.e. how the twins were treated at home and how they dressed. He does not deal with between-family environmental differences for MZ and DZ twins and siblings because these are obviously not so important. There was no need for him to specify the type of the differences he adduced because their very nature made this clear. But he would not have gone as far as Eysenck does in speaking of 'the complete absence' of between-family variance. The degree to which twins are dressed alike may vary with socioeconomic status.

In sum, Kamin is not guilty of any 'change of stance' in a logical or methodological sense. He just quotes different types of environmental influence which tend to affect the types of twin study in different ways. It is difficult to see why Eysenck makes so much of this point; he does not thereby detract from Kamin's evidence or invalidate his argument.

Fulker's criticism of Kamin (environmental similarity of twins)

The second aspect of the studies of separated twins on which Fulker takes issue with Kamin is that of similarity of environment (named by him 'selective placement', a term usually reserved for placement through an agency). Kamin shows that the IQ correlation for the 27 twin-pairs reared in related homes was 0.83 compared with only 0.51 for those in unrelated homes. Fulker assumes that those placed with relatives would be environmentally in the position of cousins, and compares their correlation of 0.83 with the 0.25 usually found for cousin-correlations, which is a powerful argument. As for the lower correlation of those in unrelated homes, he points out that they contained the three very discrepant cases; without them the correlation would be 0.84. This again raises the question of the extent to which it is permissible to selectively exclude cases incompatible with one's hypothesis. Nevertheless Fulker's main argument stands that the correlations for both groups of twins were considerably higher than those of cousins, between whom can be assumed – besides a 25 per cent sharing of genes – a certain communality of cultural environment. Kamin does not answer this point in the debate. It must be noted, however, that on this issue again Fulker does not accuse Kamin of any error of statistics but only one of interpretation.

The evidence of adoption studies

Eysenck uses two aspects of adoption studies as bases for quantitative estimates of the heritability of intelligence.

First, he argues that correlation between the IQs of the adoptive parents and their foster-children are, *in the absence of selective placement*, a direct estimate of the effects of home environment. He quotes a figure of 0.19 as a median correlation derived from several studies, which is compared with the 0.50 correlation between parents and their natural children. From the difference of about 0.3 Eysenck arrives at a 62 per cent heritability, which like all such is corrected upwards for unreliability. Eysenck does not name the studies, but in his 1979 book he gives the six from which the above overall median is obtained. They were: (1) Burks (1928), (2) Freeman *et al.* (1928), (3) Leahy (1935), (4) Horn *et al.* (1979) and (5) (6) two by Scarr and Weinberg (1978). They are listed here since they come under the detailed scrutiny of Kamin.

Kamin (p. 117) makes a general criticism of parent/child IQ correlations in adoption studies on the grounds of restricted variance: adoptive parents have been selected by agencies as especially fit people who would provide better than average environments for their children, and would consequently have higher than average IQs. There is thus a reduced amount of variability to form the basis of a correlation. He takes the analogy of boxing, in which there would be a high correlation between success and weight if there were no weight divisions. These, however, ensure that there is very little difference in the weights of boxers matched against each other, so that weight does not count for much. Kamin argues that adoptive parents are in the equivalent of one boxer-division, and that this could account for the low correlations between them and their adopted children. He does not quote evidence for the superiority of foster parents as a group.

This, however, is very apparent in two studies which compare the occupational levels of foster-fathers with State or US averages. In the Freeman (1928) study, No. 2 in the list, 15 per cent of the foster-parents were in the highest (professional) class compared with three per cent of all Illinois males; only one per cent were common labourers compared with an all-Illinois eight per cent. In the Skodak–Skeels (1949) study, quoted elsewhere by Eysenck, 14 per cent of the foster-fathers were in the highest occupational class (3.1 per cent for all USA) while none were in the lowest class consisting of day labourers (all USA 19.5 per cent) and only five per cent were in the next-lowest class (all USA 11.3 per cent).

If the low foster-parent/foster-child correlations quoted by Eysenck can be attributed to the restricted IQ variance within an occupationally superior group, the same effect should also produce low correlations between the IQs of the foster-parents and those of their biological children. Two of the studies quoted by Eysenck (No. 4 and 6) show this. In that by Horn *et al.* (1979) the IQ correlations between the foster-mothers and their natural children was 0.20, between the latter and the foster-fathers 0.28. In the Scarr–Weinberg (1977) study the corresponding figures are 0.34 and 0.34. These must be compared with the 0.5 correlation between parents and children usually found in unselected families. Kamin's explanation in terms of restricted variance thus holds up in an independent test.

Eysenck quotes a number of correlations from Burks (1928) showing a much greater resemblance of natural (non-foster) parents and their own children than of foster-parents and their adopted children (as regards IQ, 0.52 as compared with 0.20), which difference he claims must constitute a measure of the genetic factor. Kamin counters by pointing out that the effect of restricted variance did not apply to the natural parents because they were an independent sample not selected as foster-parents. Moreover their matching with the adopting parents had been far from satisfactory since the mean income of the adoptive parents was 50 per cent higher than that of the natural parents.

The second aspect of adoption studies which Eysenck adduces as evidence of a large genetic factor, and one widely regarded as demonstrating the inheritance of intelligence, is the resemblance of the adoptive children to their natural parents with whom they have had no contact since shortly after birth (p. 51). Eysenck mentions the existence of three studies in which such a resemblance was found, but quotes only one, that by Skodak and Skeels (1949). 'The pattern', he states, 'is very clear, heritability is nil when the children are two years old, but rises steadily to 80 per cent by the time they are 14. Finding that a delay *increases* the resemblance in IQ is strongly suggestive that the cause of this resemblance is genetic' (p. 51). In 1974 Kamin had published a detailed critique of the Skodak–Skeels study from the very full data given in its appendix. He showed that the natural-parent/adopted-child correlations which increased with age were based on different sample sizes, the sample being progressively reduced from 180 to 100. No conclusions, of a genetic or other nature could therefore be drawn from the progressive increase in the correlations with age. Kamin unearthed a number of other anomalies in the Skodak–Skeels findings. Although there was an overall correlation of 0.32 between the biological mother's education and her child's IQ, that for the 60 girls was 0.44, but that for the 40 boys –0.01. (Kamin 1974, p. 127). This would suggest a nil heritability for boys. As regards the relatively high correlation for the girls, the latter's IQ, and also their biological mothers' education, showed a significant negative correlation with their age (–0.31 and –0.52) which would have produced spurious correlations between the biological mother's education and their children's IQ.

Kamin's main critique of the Skodak–Skeels study is on the evidence of selective placement. The adopted children came in the main from two sources, state-supported public agencies who were legally compelled to accept all children offered by unmarried mothers, and a private agency. There were indications that the children from the private agency were placed in better adoptive homes than those placed by the public agency: among the 100 of the final sample on whom Eysenck relies for his heritability calculation, the 12 children of the least-educated biological mothers were placed with foster-mothers with two years less education than the eight children of the best-educated. The reverse also applied: the 12 foster-homes in which both parents had completed college got children of biological mothers who were two years better educated than the 22 pairs of foster-parents who had not completed high school. Kamin claims that this evidence of selective placement, together with the other anomalies in the data, offers an alternative explanation of the tendency of the IQs of adopted children to correlate with their biological mothers' IQ and education.

Although Kamin's criticisms of the Skodak–Skeels study had been published some years, Eysenck made no mention of them either in his 1979 book or in the 1981 debate. Nevertheless he continues to use their findings as the basis for his quantitative estimate of heritability. Indeed Kamin's name does not even appear in the index of the 1979 book!

The issue of selective placement is critical. For reliance to be placed on studies of adoption for the calculation of heritability it is necessary to show that the resemblance of adopted children to their natural mothers in intelligence is not a statistical artifact arising from the practice of placing agencies.

As further evidence of the effects of selection Kamin (p. 122) draws on the Scarr and Weinberg 1977 study (No. 6 in Eysenck's list). Against a correlation of 0.32 between the unmarried mother's education and the child she had had adopted, one of only 0.15 was found between her education and her child's adoptive sibling. This led the authors of the study to conclude that there was a genetic effect over and above selective placement. But Kamin, following his usual strategy of obtaining the original data, calculated that – when only those children tested on the same test (the Stanford Binet) are included – the correlation for the unmarried mother and *her child's adoptive sibling* was actually somewhat higher (0.33) than that with her own relinquished child (0.28) – despite the absence of any genetic relationship. In the study by Horn *et al.* (1979), No. 4 in Eysenck's list, the unmarried mother's IQ correlated 0.31 with her relinquished child, but only 0.08 with her child's adoptive sibling. Kamin cannot fault this finding on the grounds that different tests were used, but he quotes a correlation of 0.19 with *other* adopted children in the same family, which reflects some effect of selective placement.

Eysenck ignores these quantitative indications of the effects of selective placement, and ridicules Kamin's emphasis thereon as supposition, taking him to task for qualifying his statements with the words, *probably, likely, perhaps* (p. 166). Here Eysenck is on shaky methodological ground. Kamin can undermine Eysenck's theory merely by showing that his data can *probably* be interpreted in other ways. To quote Burt (1955), 'the defender of a hypothesis must prove that every alternative that is worth considering is *less probable* (Burt's italics) than his own'.

Eysenck's answer on the issue of selective placement is confined to the general statement that, 'in my experience none of these probabilities or possibilities accords with actual agency beliefs and practices, but in any case no argument can be based on a series of surmises without proof of any kind'. He does not say what experiences he has had with adopting agencies nor does he document their findings.

It is not difficult to find both verbal and quantitative evidence of selective placement apart from that found by Kamin in the Skodak–Skeels study. Even in this study there are indications thereof that Kamin does not quote. The correlation of the foster-parents' education with the biological mother's education was 0.27, and 0.24 with the latter's IQ. The eleven children of mothers known to be mentally retarded, with an estimated IQ of below 70, were placed in foster-homes with only half the income level of the foster-homes of the eight children of mothers who had IQs of 105 upwards. Moreover, five of these eight went to nursery schools and private schools while none of the children of mentally defective mothers did. It is of interest that these eleven children nonetheless had an average IQ of 105.4 on the five testings.

In the Burks study (1928, p. 248), No. 1 in the Eysenck list and the one whose results he quotes at greatest length, 'agencies made an attempt to place the children with foster parents whose cultural background was somewhat similar to that of the true parents.' In the Freeman *et al.* study (1928), No. 2 in the Eysenck list, the 26 children both of whose parents were mentally defective were placed in much poorer homes.

A correlation has elsewhere been noted between the criminality of adopted children and their biological fathers (Hutchings and Mednick 1977) which was likewise interpreted as a genetic effect. (The authors of this study showed that this could not have been due to the adoptive parents' knowledge of the true fathers' criminal records because the same effect obtained when the latter committed their first offences after the adoption). The authors of the study were honest enough to admit that, 'The Danish organization which arranged many of the adoptions examined in this study states clearly that they do aim at matching in certain respects'. (Hutchings and Mednick 1977 p. 138); and there was a significant correlation of 0.22 with respect to social class between the biological and adoptive parents. Nevertheless a multiple regression analysis showed that the criminality of the adopted boys was related to that of their true fathers irrespective of social class rating. This, however, could mean that the adopting agency matched by other social and personal factors. It can indeed be calculated from the table on p. 132 that the adoptees who had criminal biological fathers had a significantly greater chance, by the amount of 27 per cent, of being placed with criminal adoptive fathers. It is therefore evident that the adopting agency matched not merely by social class but by criteria of life-style which included criminality.

In sum, the alternative explanation of selective placement is based on more solid evidence than 'surmises without proof of any kind'. It would seem to be something inseparable from the adoption process, given contemporary notions of social fairness. Being, as the evidence shows, a potent yet incalculable factor, it destroys the value of adoption studies for the estimation of heritability.

Fulker's criticism of Kamin (adoption studies)

Fulker makes no attempt to defend the Freeman, Holzinger and Mitchell study, which he describes as 'replete with problems of separation and selective placement' and lacking a control group

(p. 512). He does, however, take up Kamin's criticism of the Burks and Leahy studies to the effect that the adoptive and control families were not matched for parental age, wealth or number of children in the family. Fulker agrees that these omissions are not trivial, but considers that they could not override mental age and occupational status, for which the two groups of families were matched. He attributes the 50 per cent higher income of the adoptive parents to the fact that they were older; he has nothing to say about the 63 per cent of the adoptees who were only children (Kamin 1974, p. 118). As regards the effects of the defective matching, Fulker is pitting his judgment against that of Kamin: he is not accusing him of statistical error.

On the question of the restricted variance of IQ in foster-homes as a selected segment of the population, Fulker asks why in this case there is not a much smaller standard deviation among foster-children compared with those in natural families. In the Leahy study the SDs were in effect 12.5 for the foster-children and 15.4 for the controls, which according to Kamin is significant. Fulker considers this a 'small restriction'. (But to find a significant difference at all with so many other uncontrolled variables must be accounted something). The greater amount of congenital damage found in adopted children (Stott 1976) and their much greater liability to behaviour disturbance as shown in criminality studies (Hutchings and Mednick 1977) would tend to enlarge the variance, if – as must be the case – only a certain proportion of the children are affected. Kamin attributes the lack of any difference in IQ variance among the Burks adoptees to some such effect, pointing out that they included a relatively large number of children with very low IQs (Kamin 1974 p. 121). Fulker disputes this, alleging that the mean and the median were the same among the adoptees and controls. Reference to the original report of the study shows that the mean for the adoptees was 107.4 but that for the controls 115.4. Of the adoptees 7.9 per cent had IQs of 89 or less compared with only 1.9 per cent of the controls; there were three adoptees but no controls with 69 or below. On these points of fact Kamin seems to be correct.

Kamin quotes correlations taken from three adoption studies showing (pp. 123–4 and Table 9) that the true children of adoptive parents do not resemble their parents in IQ significantly more than do the adoptive children. He draws the conclusion that, 'within adoptive families, it *makes no difference* whether or not the child shares the parent's genes. There seems to be no plausible hereditarian way to explain this finding.' (p. 124). Fulker rises to the challenge, and for the reader to follow his argument it is necessary to reproduce his Table 5 as Table 2 (see page 51). The first three columns are taken from that of Kamin, the fourth is added by Fulker. Kamin bases his argument on a comparison of columns 1 and 2. He rejects column 3, the traditional comparison, because of the inadequate matching and the atypicality leading to restricted variance of adoptive families. Fulker's column 4 relates to the small subset of adoptive parents who have a true child, but refers to the 26 adopted children in those families. Fulker claims that these represent the appropriate comparisons with the natural control children of column 3. However, Kamin has already listed his objections to these controls, and Fulker should only have claimed that his column 4 was a more accurate comparison with the children's adoptive siblings of column 2. In a rather confused exposition he goes on to compare the children of columns 2 and 4, so that 'column 3' is possibly a misprint. He admits that among these two groups of children living in the adopting families there is 'a genuine reduction in the range of IQ determinants'. Making an approximate correction for this, he arrives at a correlation of 0.51 for the adoptive parents with their own offspring, and 0.29 with their adopted children.

It should be noted that this calculation is in respect of a small sub-sample within the Freeman study only, which Fulker had previously left out of consideration as too contaminated with age of adoption and selective placement. Reference to the original study (Freeman, Holzinger and Mitchell 1928) reveals that it was in no sense a natural experiment in taking children from near birth and placing them in a different environment. The mean age of committal to the institution from which the adoptions were effected was 4 years 5 months. But the sample was made up of two groups, illegitimate children who were committed very young, and legitimate children – nearly all from immoral, breakdown families – who were committed late. There were over twice as many legitimate as illegitimate children in the sample, so that a good proportion, if not the majority of the 26 on which Fulker based his calculation, would have been children taken into private families at too late an age to be compared with the adoptive parents' own children. For approximately half their lives up to the time of testing this legitimate group had been living in families from which they had had to be rescued. Apart from the postnatal privations and deprivations from which they must have suffered, their family settings were of the type typically associated with high interpersonal stresses likely to produce congenital damage (seen chiefly as a high prevalence of 'subcultural' feeble mindedness). Of the legitimate, problem-family group 24.3 per cent had an IQ of 79 or less compared with only 6.8 per cent of the illegitimate group. Such a large proportion of mentally subnormal children at the lower end of the distribution would increase the variance upon which Fulker presumably based his correction, but as a random factor completely independent of the adoptive-parents' influence it would also have reduced the resemblance between the latter and their adopted children. No further examination of the real state of affairs in this subsample is needed to show that it offers no basis for the calculation of correlations, let alone of heritability.

IQ comparisons of blood relations

The third source of evidence upon which Eysenck relies consists in comparisons of IQs of blood relatives. He claims that 'the results are astonishingly close to what one would expect from a simple model in which IQ is largely inherited and environment has a small influence' (namely that genetic factors account for some 70 per cent, corrected to 80 per cent, of individual differences in intelligence). Disappointingly, Eysenck devotes a mere 12 lines (p. 51) to this part of his thesis and quotes no evidence or sources. In his 1979 book he used the Erlenmeyer–Kimling and Jarvik study (1963) – for short EKJ – 'augmented in cases where numbers were small and critical studies have since been carried out' (p. 115). He did not, however, add to the 12 studies of natural parents and their children, for which EKJ gave a median correlation of 0.50, exactly what would be genetically predicted (p. 113). Kamin (p. 137) describes this median as artificial because of the wide variability of the results (from 0.2 to about 0.8). Moreover he located 16 studies carried out since 1963, the year of publication of the EKJ summary. In them the median parent–child correlation was only 0.33, with individual values varying from 0.08 to 0.41. He stressed that not a single one reached the level of the 0.50 median of the earlier studies. This new median, Kamin avers, 'would wreak havoc on the models used by the hereditarians' (p. 136). He calculates that three recent studies, those of DeFries (1979), Spuhler (1976) and Guttman (1974), indicate heritabilities respectively of 25, 13 and 26 per cent. His main contention, however, is that all such parent–child correlations could be explained by an environmental model because, being closely related and living together, parents and children share a common environment.

Eysenck does not answer Kamin's criticisms in detail, and does not dispute the findings of the 16 more recent studies. Instead, he accuses

Kamin of being 'very selective in his choice of examples, usually picking those which suit his thesis'. This, Eysenck (p. 165) declares is 'not accidental but intentional'. In making a serious accusation against another scholar, especially when his integrity is impugned, it is a matter of common prudence to substantiate the charge by quoting chapter and verse. This Eysenck fails to do. In fact Kamin did not ignore the earlier 12 studies summarized by EKJ; it was rather Eysenck who was guilty of selection by ignoring the 16 more recent ones. The only support that Eysenck quotes for his accusation is Kamin's reference to 'artificial median correlations'. Eysenck then proceeds to justify the median as a statistical concept as if Kamin had objected to the use of the median in general. But in using the word 'artificial' Kamin was referring to particular medians, those quoted by EKJ, on the ground that they disguised widely varying correlations.

Fulker's criticism of Kamin
1. The Erlenmeyer–Kimling and Jarvik diagram

Kamin directs his scrutiny on to the EKJ diagram, summarizing the correlations reported in 52 studies, which is the foundation of Eysenck's case for a mainly genetic determination of IQ. Its authors did not, surprisingly, list the 52 studies. Kamin, however, succeeded in obtaining them from Jarvik. Perusal of the studies left him uninformed about which of the reported correlations had been selected for inclusion in the diagram. Some articles dealt with more than one sample, and gave both raw correlations and corrections for unreliability, restricted range, and age. In a later article Jarvik and Erlenmeyer–Kimling merely stated that the table included the original investigators' best estimates. But Kamin quotes one in which this is not the case.

Fulker offers no answer to these criticisms, but regards Kamin's discarding of the adoption and MZ twin studies included in the EKJ diagram as 'almost totally unjustified' since they provide 'powerful and direct evidence of a strong genetic influence on IQ'. Fulker writes as if this exclusion was arbitrary, but a large part of Kamin's 1974 book is taken up with his reasons for rejecting them.

2. Siblings reared apart

Fulker's concern was that the elimination of the MZ twin and adoption studies left only two, those of full sibs reared apart, as providing such direct evidence of a strong genetic influence. The studies in question were one by Freeman *et al.* (1928) and one by Burt (1955). The latter study has since been discredited. The Freeman study gives two correlations, 0.34 and 0.25, arrived at by different methods. EKJ chose the first, but Kamin argues that, to be consistent with the one they used from Burt, they should have chosen the second. Kamin also discovered among the EKJ references a study by Hildreth (1925) which reported on 78 full sibs reared apart, which, however, was not included in the EKJ diagram. It gave a raw correlation of only 0.23, boosted by Hildreth to 0.50 owing to restricted range. Even allowing for such, Kamin claimed the corrected figure should be 0.28, but since there was in fact no restricted range among the separated sibs, the original correlation of 0.23 was the true one. The importance of this correlation is that whereas a correlation of 0.40 to which Burt's of 0.46 would have brought the median value suggests strong genetic determination, one of 0.25 could have been produced by the rearing of the siblings in similar environments without postulating a genetic factor. This particular controversy is now academic since Burt's work is no longer accepted. Fulker describes Kamin's treatment of the issue as 'arbitrary', although Kamin gave his reasons for the choice of the lower correlation. Fulker does not maintain that he is in error.

Sex linkage

Eysenck adduces three types of demographic evidence for the genetic transmission of 'intelligence'. The first is that of sex linkage, suggested by the well-known tendency for the distribution of IQ scores for males to be spread more into the extremes while that for females is bunched nearer to the average. He reproduces Lehrke's (1978) argument that this is due to the male's having only one x-chromosome, so that there is no second one to 'reduce the impact of whatever genetic information is contained in the first' (Eysenck p. 43). Lehrke quotes a great amount of evidence to show that there is an excess of mental retardation among males, and it is well known that males are more liable to nearly all types of non-infectious disease and physical defect. He is, however, at pains to show that the greater IQ variability of males is not merely a matter of pathology: males are over-represented also at the higher end of the distribution, as shown in Terman's sample of bright children. The weakness of the theory is precisely this excess of very high IQ males. If, as Eysenck claims on page 65, the genes for 'high intelligence' are dominant over those for 'low intelligence', we have to ask why the second female x-chromosome should 'reduce the impact' of the homologous gene which contributes to 'high intelligence'. Lehrke similarly skips over this difficulty, merely stating that the single male x-chromosome is free to act "at full force, whether deleterious, beneficial or neutral" (Lehrke 1978, p. 174).

The debate between Eysenck and Kamin on this issue of sex linkage in the genetic determination of 'intelligence' centres on correlations quoted by Lehrke from Bayley (1966) of intra-familial IQs. Bayley selected from Outhit's (1933) data those in which there were scores for mother and father plus a son and a daughter. The father–son correlation was only 0.44, while the other three permutations were 0.61,

0.66 and 0.68. Lehrke argues that this supports his theory, since the sons would not have shared any x-chromosomes with their fathers; what father–son resemblance there was must have been due to the resemblance, as regards intelligence, of the mothers to the fathers. Eysenck (p. 43) claims on the basis of Lehrke's argument, supported by the Bayley correlations, that, 'We are now in a position to suggest that male–female differences in IQ variability may have a genetic basis in sex-linkage'.

Kamin attacks this sex-linkage claim on two counts. First, he points out – what neither Lehrke nor Eysenck mention – that Bayley's correlations were drawn from only 51 families; and he was formally correct in stating that none of the correlations were significant (although, according to Bayley, they approached the 0.05 level). Second, Kamin (pp. 173–4) quotes eleven more recent studies, in all of which the samples were larger than 51. These fail to support the x-chromosome hypothesis. In three the father/son correlation is actually the highest; and the mean ranks of the father/son and mother/son correlations are almost equal. There seems, therefore, to be nothing more than a chance relationship between them. (Sex linkage has appeared in the controversy since Kamin's 1974 book was published, so that there is no reference to it in Fulker's 1975 critical review).

Inbreeding depression

Eysenck's second line of demographic evidence is again based on his postulate that the genes for 'high intelligence' are dominant. This means that 'in consanguineous marriages the recessive genes which lower intelligence have less chance of being offset by dominant ones. Recessive genes are more likely to pair up, thereby depressing intelligence' (p. 66). Several large-scale studies of cousin marriages, Eysenck claims, have demonstrated this effect. Apart from mentioning their location in Japan and among Arabs in Israel, he does not indicate which studies he is referring to. In his 1979 book (p. 123), however, he quotes the Schull and Neel (1965) Japanese study, and that of Bashi (1977) of Israeli Arabs.

By way of answer, Kamin (p. 144) draws attention to the finding by Schull and Neel that the cousins who had married had significantly lower socioeconomic status than unrelated couples, and would on that account have had lower IQs. In his 1979 book (p. 123) Eysenck admitted the 'confounding effects of age and social class which mimicked inbreeding depression', and hinted at statistical corrections which 'have caused a certain amount of doubt concerning the outcome of their (Schull and Neel's) study'. In the 1981 debate he nonetheless makes no mention of such doubts. With regard to Bashi's study of Israeli Arabs, Kamin points out that the 1-2 IQ point inferiority of children of cousin marriages was not properly controlled for social-class effects and that such marriages are probably more common in the country than in the towns, where IQ scores would be lower. Kamin consequently does not agree with Eysenck's conclusion 'That these studies of inbreeding depression confirm that for many of the genes influencing IQ there is a marked degree of dominance. Our idea of the genetic architecture of intelligence is that much clearer' (p. 66).

Eysenck goes on to estimate, on the basis of the inbreeding–depression studies 'and other methods' that about 50 genes are involved in the determination of differences in intelligence.

Regression to the mean

Eysenck's third category of demographic evidence for the preponderant genetic element in 'intelligence' is that children born to the most able and successful tend to regress towards the mean, while the children of the dullest and least successful regress upwards, despite the environmental influences which should act in the opposite directions. This phenomenon, Eysenck maintains, 'offers impressive proof of the contribution of genetic factors' and 'poses enormous difficulties for any environmentalist explanation of individual differences in IQ'. He knows of no attempt to explain it in environmental terms, and 'Kamin dismisses the phenomenon as if it had never existed' (p. 162).

Kamin does not in effect treat the phenomenon as if it had never existed. He points out (p. 180) that regression is a 'necessary *statistical* consequence of the simple fact that the correlation in IQ between parent and child is less than perfect'. This indeed is a statistical commonplace. In the chapters in which Jensen (1980) explains the statistical basis of his concept of intelligence – which is the same as that of Eysenck – he emphasizes (p. 189) precisely Kamin's point; there are always factors which prevent the extreme instances of a variable x being correspondingly extreme in the variable y, and conversely the extreme instances of variable y will not be fully reflected in the corresponding instances of variable x. Kamin points out (p. 180) that this two-way feature of regression to the mean requires that the IQs of parents of high IQ children will inevitably not be as high as those of their children; yet no one would suggest that the parents inherited their intelligence from their children! In short, the regression phenomenon carries no genetic implications.

The influence of environment

Eysenck makes it clear that he does not deny all environmental influence on intelligence. He is willing to accord it up to 20 per cent of the variance. This enables him to claim that mean gains in IQ of 20 points as in the Heber experiment (pp. 57–8) or of 16 points in the Schiff study (p. 164) are compatible with his estimate of an 80 per cent genetic contribution to IQ differences.

The French study by Schiff *et al.* (1978) found that the IQs of 32 lower working-class children adopted into economically superior homes were considerably higher, 111 compared to 95, than those of 20 of their siblings who remained with their own parents. Kamin quoted this result as an example of how IQ can be boosted by a more favourable environment. Eysenck uses it as an example of Kamin's 'incredible errors' (p. 164), reading into it 'the erroneous assumption that the genetic hypothesis requires almost complete absence of environmental determination' (p. 165). In effect Kamin merely quoted the study as an example of a significant environmental effect, without implying that the genetic hypothesis ruled out any environmental effect. In view of his detailed examination of the various heritability models (pp. 137–9) it is difficult to see how his use of the Schiff result could carry the erroneous implication that Eysenck attributes to it.

Eysenck goes on to use Kamin's reference to the Schiff study as an example of his 'failure to take a proper quantitative look at the evidence' (p. 164). It is, however, questionable whether a study with such a small number of subjects, with sibling pairs of different ages and pre-selected by unknown criteria for adoption, can bear the weight of a heritability computation. Kamin (who could not reply to Eysenck's stricture because it was in the latter's rejoinder) would certainly also have something to say about a formula which equated a 16 point IQ gain with only a 20 per cent share of the variance for environment. One has to ask what IQ boost would be required to produce a 50 per cent share. If it is in proportion it would be one of 40 points, which, added to the original mean of 95, would amount to an IQ for the adopted children of 135. One would have to search a long time to find such an *average* level among any group of educationally unselected children, even in the most favourable of environments.

Finally, to use the Schiff results as the basis for a heritability calculation carries the assumption that there were no common features in the environments of each sibling pair. It is overlooked that the period of gestation and the first six months of life were lived with the same mother and the same family setting. Ongoing interpersonal stresses during the pregnancy, especially marital discord, double the risk of morbidity in the child (Stott 1973; Stott and Latchford 1976). This includes the child's temperamental stability, which would in turn impair mental development (Stott 1981). Chronic illnesses during pregnancy, such as respiratory and digestive disease, are associated with between a 50 and 75 per cent greater prevalence of childhood morbidity. All these prenatal risks are very much higher in disadvantaged families such as those from which the children of the Schiff study were taken, and the fact that the parents allowed one of their children to be adopted suggests that they had more than their share of family troubles. It is reasonable also to suppose that in disadvantaged families there would be a greater prevalence of early postnatal malnutrition and faulty health care. In short, both the adopted children and their non-adopted siblings in the Schiff study shared a similar environment during gestation and early infancy, which, at least in animal studies, have been found to be highly determinative for later development (Smart 1977).

Moreover, it cannot be assumed that the relinquishment of the children for adoption in the Schiff study was a random business. Almost certainly the parents would have tended to retain the bonnier, better-behaved and developmentally more forward babies. Consequently those relinquished for adoption would as a group have had a poorer prognosis for mental development. The 16-point superiority of the adopted children over their retained siblings is thus all the more noteworthy.

That both the adoptees and the non-adoptees shared a common, disadvantaged environment during their early lives, and that this carried with it a major risk of congenital and early postnatal damage, must have had the statistical effect of reducing the variance of their IQs. In practical terms, the greater proportion of chronic health, neurological and temperamental problems from which they were likely to have suffered would have meant that some of them, even in the most favourable environments, would have had limited possibilities for improvement in their IQ. The extent of such constitutional damage among lower working-class children is brought out clearly in the second report of the National Child Development Study (Davie, Butler and Goldstein 1972, pp. 460–79 and 366–78) and in Stott, Marston and Neill (1975, pp. 94–95) for Canadian children. The tables on those pages show how children of fathers of occupational group V (unskilled labourers) and of parents living in poor homes stand out as the most impaired group as regards behaviour disturbance, speech development, walking and manual control. The greatest deficits were in those types of motivation, unforthcomingness and inconsequence, most detrimental to mental development. No allowance is made for these constitutional, but nonetheless environmental, factors making for restricted variance in the heritability formulas. Kamin has not so far appreciated the extent to which the powerful formative influences of the prenatal and early-infancy periods detract from the validity of all adoption studies as measures of heritability, but there were many cogent reasons apart from them for not attempting to fit the Schiff findings into a heritability formula. His refraining from doing so can hardly be described, as Eysenck does (p. 164) as 'an incredible statistical error'.

In support of his claim that environment exercises only a minor influence Eysenck selects two studies, that by Lawrence of orphanage children, and that by Firkowska of Warsaw children reared in similar neighbourhoods.

Eysenck argues (p. 53) that if the environment is the sole determinant of mental development there should be little if any variability in the IQs of orphanage children, since an orphanage 'provides as identical an environment as it is humanly possible to produce'. If on the other hand genetic factors are the chief determinant, the range of IQ in orphanage children should be only slightly lower than that of children brought up by their own parents. Eysenck quotes the Lawrence (1931) study as finding little shrinkage in the range of IQs among orphanage children. He admits that the number of children in the study 'was not large enough to make the conclusions compelling' (pp. 53–4). Nevertheless he generalizes from it to write, 'studies of this kind are of particular importance from the social point of view because they indicate the limitations of egalitarian social policies in producing greater equality of IQ'.

Kamin (pp. 148–9) disputes Eysenck's basic assumption that the children in Lawrence's orphanage study had had a virtually identical environment. They had not been given up by their mothers until they were six months old on average, and up to the age of five or six years they had been boarded out in individual foster-homes. In his reply (p. 162) Eysenck points out that he had earlier admitted that 'too much may have been made of these findings' (the Lawrence study). Nonetheless he continued to maintain (pp. 79–80) that this and the Warsaw study disproved the environmental hypothesis.

The feature of the Warsaw study (Firkowska 1978), was that, after the wartime destruction of the city, the rebuilt dwellings were allocated without regard to social class. All the children were therefore exposed to the same *extrinsic* (between-family) environment in the form of similar accommodation, schools, health facilities, shopping centres and so on. Only their *intrinsic*, inner-family environment differed. The test results showed no relation to the extrinsic factors, but a strong, even relationship with parental occupation and education – 'very much as it would in a typical capitalist society' (p. 54). Eysenck claims that this study produced 'results very similar to those observed in the small-scale orphanage study', namely that 'both in turn strongly support the relative roles assigned to genetic and environmental factors . . . on the basis of twin and family studies' (p. 55).

In his very brief reference to the Warsaw study Kamin merely queries the near-uniform character of the extrinsic environment. He neglects to point out that an important within-family environment remained, which the study did not isolate from the genetic factors. It is difficult to see how Eysenck could have reached any conclusion from it on the relative roles of heredity and environment.

Biological counterparts of IQ

Eysenck is confident that there must be underlying physiological reasons for innate differences in ability. He tells us that, 'Recent work, some of it not yet published, has indeed begun to identify these physiological mechanisms and to measure them with considerable success. It provides the most convincing proof to date of the correctness of the genetic model of intelligence' (p. 67). This is a large claim, and the reader has a right to expect convincing 'hard' evidence for a biological intelligence. That proffered by Eysenck consists of findings on reaction times, and EEG evoked potentials.

Reaction times

For reaction times Eysenck relies on the work of Jensen, 'who has been able to show that the hypothetical speed of nervous transmission measured in this way is quite highly correlated with intelligence as measured by traditional IQ tests' (p. 67). Eysenck does not give the actual correlations, so that reference has to be made to Jensen (1980).

Apart from his own recent, and admittedly exploratory work, the only previous study that Jensen can quote showing a significant correlation of IQ and reaction time was that by Lemmon in the 1920s. Even then, the correlation was a modest one of 0.25 and applied to choice reaction only. Moreover Lemmon was working in the laboratory of J. McK. Cattell, who was committed to the search for physiological explanations of psychological phenomena. Such a setting contains powerful temptations to bias, if only in the continued rejection of non-significant findings.

Jensen likewise found no correlation between IQ and simple reaction time, i.e. when the subject responds to the sound-signal by pressing the same button every time. With the apparatus on which he obtained his results the subject had to respond by pressing one of up to eight buttons as randomly indicated by a light. The mental processes involved were therefore more than the sheer speed of conduction along nerve paths. To be able to make any of a variety of responses at short notice requires the use of cognitive strategies, namely flexibility in keeping all alternatives open and avoiding expectancies, and intense concentration. Whereas it could be argued that these are constituents of intelligence, the subject's state of health, temperament and cultural conditioning must also play a part (as applies to all complex behaviours including test performance). And indeed Jensen found his subjects' median reaction times 'highly unstable from day to day', thus showing considerable shifts in rank order (p. 691). The choice reaction times that Jensen used showed the lowest day-to-day reliability (p. 691). Moreover he found that his and his wife's reaction times showed considerable fluctuations at different times of the day, tending to slow down from morning until late afternoon (p. 692).

Jensen gives broad descriptions of seven studies of reaction time carried out in his laboratory, but for none of them does he give straight correlations with IQ. He prefers instead various equivalents, such as the slope of the regression lines relative to each other, and the mean standard deviations at the four levels of task complexity, calculated to confuse and overawe the statistically uninitiated. Even for the correlations thus obtained, which he claims are significantly correlated with IQ, he gives no precise values. Essentially he bases the existence of a *g*-component on the demonstration of an increase in reaction time as a linear function of the logarithm of the number of choices. This applied with all the samples except that of the severely retarded (p. 692). However, all he gives by way of results is a graph showing six straight regression lines and one bent one (Figure 14.13). He explains (p. 695) that 'for the sake of graphical clarity, I have plotted the regression lines without the data points'. In fact it would have been easy to indicate these by the use of symbols.

The only one of the correlations he reveals is that of "about −0.40" for a sample of 39 ninth-grade girls. However, from his graph (Figure 14.12) the size of these correlations can be approximately gauged for the above sample of girls and for university students. For the latter they are virtually zero until the 8-choice set-up is used. For the girls there is, against all precedent, a correlation of −0.26 between IQ and simple reaction time, and there is not a straight linear regression with increase in number of choices (−0.32, −0.40, −0.47, −0.35). In other words, with increasing complexity of choice in reaction times, there are only random changes in the correlations of the above indirect measures with IQ.

Up to the time Eysenck wrote his contribution to the debate Jensen had published no systematic account of any of the above experiments such as would allow them to be replicated outside his laboratory. We cannot be sure, therefore, that he has taken the necessary safeguards against spurious effects arising from the conditions of administration of the tests. For example, if both the reaction-time and IQ-tests were administered during the same morning and afternoon sessions for individual subjects, if some were tested at one part of the day and some at another, and if there was a general variability of performance for reaction-time and IQ-test according to the time of day, a spurious correlation would result. Jensen gives no information on time of day of testing. It could account for the suspicious correlation of –0.26 for *simple* reaction time and IQ found in the sample of girls as well as the choice reaction-time correlations.

There is a convention that no weight can be placed on findings until they are systematically reported and their procedures made available for scrutiny. Kamin asserts that he has repeatedly asked Jensen for his raw data on one study briefly reported in 1975, that in which blacks were found to be inferior to whites in complex reaction tasks, but that Jensen has repeatedly refused to supply them. (Kamin considered the finding implausible in view of the prowess of blacks at boxing and basketball). At any rate there is as yet no scientific evidence to show, as Eysenck claims on the basis of Jensen's work, 'that the hypothetical speed of nervous transmission measured (by reaction times) is quite highly correlated with intelligence as measured by traditional IQ tests' (p. 67).

EEG evoked potentials

Eysenck's own favoured means of demonstrating a physiological basis for intelligence is that of EEG evoked potentials. These are characteristic waves produced when the subject is exposed to a sudden noise or flash of light (p. 70). He quotes the finding of Ertl (Ertl and Schafer 1969) that dull subjects produced slower (more widely spaced) waves than bright ones, and reproduces Ertl's records for ten children of each type. Eysenck goes on to claim (p. 72) that, in his own laboratory, Elaine Hendrikson 'as have other people before' confirmed this finding, and by improved techniques obtained higher correlations, as high as 0.6 and 0.8, between measured intelligence and evoked potentials. Eysenck lays great weight on these results, which afford us 'direct evidence of important physiological factors closely related to cognitive functioning as measured by IQ tests. A concrete, measureable biological basis has been found for IQ'.

Kamin describes evoked potentials as a myth: neither Ertl himself or others had been able to repeat the above findings; and Elaine Hendrikson's research had never been published, although Eysenck mentioned it in an article as long ago as 1973 (p. 180). In this article, according to Kamin, Eysenck also quoted the work of Rust in his laboratory as finding very high heritabilities for evoked potentials. However, Rust's research was published in 1975. Working with a sample size three times larger than Hendrickson's, he failed to find any correlation between evoked potential and IQ (p. 181). Kamin points out that Eysenck must have known of this contradictory result when he referred to the unpublished research.

Kamin's stricture seems on the whole justified, but the facts he adduces require some clarification. In his review of previous work Rust (1975) mentions five studies apart from the series of which Ertl was a co-author that found a correlation between evoked potential and IQ. On the other hand several studies (Rust mentions five) produced contradictory results. One of these reported Ertl's failure to replicate his own findings. It is only technically accurate to say that Hendrickson's work was unpublished; as a PhD thesis of the University of London it would be available for consultation and in microfilm, so that Eysenck was justified in quoting it. However, Rust used the same procedures as Elaine Hendrikson in two studies, neither of which produced evidence for a relationship between IQ and evoked potential. To account for the contradictory findings of the various studies, Rust suggests that the significant correlations were due to unknown intervening variables, or to 'the well-known literature bias in favour of positive results'. He concludes that, 'we would not be justified in basing any theory of personality or IQ in terms of biological variables on generalized results from evoked potential data'. Kamin quotes Jensen's (1980) reference to the work on evoked potentials as 'a thicket of seemingly inconsistent and confusing findings'.

Fulker re-states the hereditarian case

The remainder of Fulker's review is taken up, not with specific criticisms of Kamin, but with an attempt to vindicate the hereditarian case. He argues that the correlation of 0.9 obtained for MZ twins reared together – which is close to the test-retest correlation for the same person – cannot be even plausibly due to their similarity of environment; and if environment had all that influence we ought to be able to discover its nature by comparing the environments of different sets of MZ twins. Fulker further argues that, since separated MZ twins no longer have the special environment created by each other's companionship, their greater resemblance in IQ compared with DZs reared together is hard to explain environmentally. Kamin would of course counter that – owing to the incompleteness of separation, similarity of environment, age bias in test scores and tester-bias – no reliance can be placed on the studies of twins reared apart. He claims that these sources of bias *could* account for the different correlations; he has not shown that they do. It still has to be shown how IQ can be changed massively in ordinary families by different treatments. Such studies would have to reckon with the observation made by virtually all parents of how different in temperament and attitudes to achievement their own children are, despite a very similar cultural background and upbringing, and that such differences usually go back to the earliest years. My own view is that, since differences in health, temperament and motivation are likely to be genetically conditioned and must have a large influence on mental development, the genetic identity of MZ twins must be reflected in some similarity of performance on mental tests.

Having made this cogent point Fulker nevertheless insists on pinning his faith to the traditional evidence that Kamin had so devastatingly attacked. This involves him in further manipulation of data and approximate, unsubstantiated estimates of the size of the various factors which detract from the accuracy of the quantitative estimation of heritability. Feeling that he has to answer a disturbing statistic in the Freeman study, that the differences in IQ of their MZ twins reared apart correlate highly (+79) with the quality of their education, he indulges in his previous device of excluding the four pairs (out of a mere 19) which are mainly responsible for this correlation. Surely this is like the batsman who objects to being out because the bowler bowled an unusually tricky ball.

Fulker then devises a revised heritability model which he claims allows for the imperfections of the data base. This entails his using the findings of Freeman *et al.* (1928) on full sibs reared apart, despite his previous characterization of this study as 'replete with problems of separation and selective placement' (p. 512). He corrects their correlation for MZ twins reared apart for gross differences in educational and social background *by removing the four most affected pairs*. He compensates for the effects of selective placement, insufficient separation, age biases, special MZ twin environment, and gross effects of a common educational, social and home background, in his Table 7, by a weighting of zero or one, which must be guesswork. The outcome is that he is able to reestablish a genetic model, concluding that, 'The cumulative picture is overwhelmingly in favour of a substantial heritability of IQ'.

It seems incongruous that, in contrast to his meticulous and reasoned criticisms of Kamin, Fulker in his concluding paragraph reverts to sweeping denunciations: Kamin is ill-informed, lacks balanced judgment and 'presents a travesty of the empirical evidence'; by exaggerating the importance of idiosyncratic details he 'totally avoids the necessity to consider the data as a whole'. It is these concluding remarks that Eysenck echoes and enlarges upon. The truth is that nowhere has Fulker revealed any 'almost incredible statistical errors', or indeed any statistical errors of any degree in Kamin's work. The issues between them have been in the value each placed on the data, the interpretation of the findings of the various studies, and the estimation of effects about which we have all too little evidence for the formation of confident judgments.

Eysenck's counterattack

Eysenck concedes that Kamin has discovered 'a number of anomalies in the literature', but claims that these merely indicate the need for better research (p. 163). He does not say which of these 'anomalies' he accepts or rejects, explaining that, 'although the temptation to answer Kamin's criticisms in detail, pointing out the way in which quotations are wrenched out of context, misinterpreted and generally abused, is almost irresistible, I will not give way to it, but concentrate rather on the factual points directly relevant to the great intelligence debate itself.' (p. 158). It is a great pity that Eysenck took so self-denying a stance, because in a debate points not answered go by default. Kamin raised many 'factual points' which merited his attention.

Eysenck further explains that, 'It is impossible, for reasons of length, to go through Kamin's whole presentation with a fine-tooth comb, pointing out all the fundamental errors, mistaken assumptions, erroneous statistics, invalid arguments, and downright falsehoods' (p. 166). These are serious accusations, and it is customary in academic disputation to document such with very great care. On the question of space, of the 78 pages of his main contribution Eysenck devotes the first 32 to what can only be described as elementary psychometric textbook material, many of the figures in which are in any case identical with those in his 1979 book. He would have done better to use this space to forestall the arguments which Kamin, to judge by his earlier attacks on the hereditarian position, would be likely to use.

Eysenck's general criticism of Kamin is that he concentrated on finding faults in individual studies but failed 'to take a proper quantitative look at the evidence' (p. 164), notably the 'quantitative agreement between estimates of heritability derived from wholly different approaches' (p. 162). Eysenck is referring to the mathematical models designed to arrive at general estimates of the relative 'contributions' of heredity and environment.

Kamin in effect devotes a whole chapter (pp. 134–9) to these models, and makes two general criticisms of them. The first is that their mathematical cleverness cannot compensate for data that are falsified or of poor quality. He devotes a large part of his contribution to the demonstration that the studies of twins, adopted children and kinship, which provided the main data for these models, were too unreliable to provide a basis for the calculation of heritability. And he took up a large part of his 1974 book in demonstrating the worthlessness of Burt's twin data, a fact that has since been generally recognized. It was not, therefore, a matter of Kamin's concentrating on 'individual studies' to the neglect of the overall, quantitative picture: in his critique of the latter he set out to destroy its foundations.

Kamin further argues that, even if the data were reliable and they fitted a genetic model, they could well also fit an environmental model (p. 134). Close relatives can have similar IQs because they live together and share the same culture and environment just as much as because they share some of the same genes. Consequently the fit of data to a genetic model does not prove a predominant genetic determination so long as the genetic determination of the constituent data remains unproved. If this is not the case, interpretation lies in the eye of the beholder.

Kamin goes on to make a number of specific criticisms of the various statistical models of heritability. These can be summarized. Model makers have lumped together, in the form of average or median correlations, the results of many different investigations using samples drawn from different populations tested by different tests. Moreover, each model maker arbitrarily chose different investigations. The median correlations disguised wide discrepancies in the correlations found for each kinship comparison. More recent studies have produced much lower correlations which do not fit a genetic model (p. 136); and these studies have not been incorporated into any of the models. Two well-known models, those devised by Jinks and Fulker in Birmingham and Eaves in Honolulu, used only the Burt correlations, which have since been shown to be fraudulent. Few model makers allowed for the possibility that IQ correlations between relatives could reflect common culture and environment, and those who did admit such covariance allocated arbitrary, and small, effects thereto. The Birmingham and Honolulu models make the assumptions that the experiences of MZ twins are no more similar than those of ordinary siblings, that there was no selective placement of adopted children, and that the adopting families were a typical cross-section of the population.

In sum, Kamin dealt with the various quantitative estimates of heritability both methodologically and as regards the reliability of their data bases. Eysenck can hardly claim that he 'leaves completely unexplained the quantitative agreement found between many different avenues of approach to the problem of estimating the heritability of intelligence' (p. 171). It has also to be noted, for the weighing of argument and counter-argument in the debate, that Eysenck in his rejoinder did not answer any of Kamin's criticisms of the models, but limited himself to the above general statements as if Kamin's chapter had never been written.

Apart from accusing Kamin of neglecting the 'quantitative argument' (p. 162), the main thrust of Eysenck's rejoinder is directed against his scholarly competence and personal integrity. He makes the charge that Kamin does not look at all the research literature, and 'completely passes over relevant evidence contrary to his position' (p. 161). As examples of the latter Eysenck quotes the issues of regression to the mean, the Lawrence and Warsaw studies, reaction times and evoked potentials. In effect there was little of Eysenck's evidence that Kamin passed over unanswered, and he did in fact deal with each of the five areas which Eysenck lists in support of his accusation. He neatly dismissed the phenomenon of the regression of children's IQ scores to the mean as a necessary feature of all correlation. He subjected the Lawrence orphanage study to close scrutiny, showing that the children's environments were not uniform enough to assume that the observed IQ variability must have been genetic. He did, however, deal with the Warsaw study rather cavalierly, merely querying the uniformity of the inter-family environment; he omitted to point out that the within-family environments of the children must have been subject to socioeconomic and cultural variations, so that, despite Eysenck's using it as evidence for heredity, the study had no relevance to the genetic-environmental issue.

As regards reaction times, it is true that Kamin limited himself to attempts to get Jensen's raw data, but Eysenck in turn accepted Jensen's inadequately reported findings uncritically and made them sound definitive enough to bear the weight of theory-building. In the matter of evoked potentials, it was rather Eysenck who passed over relevant evidence contrary to his position.

In sum, Eysenck still has to substantiate his charges against Kamin, amounting to gross academic incompetence, intention misrepresentation and falsehood, by better evidence than he quotes in the debate. Indeed some of his accusations could backfire on himself. Apart from his overlooking of Rust's findings on evoked potentials, he took no account of those contrary to his thesis on the kinship studies subsequent to the EKJ tabulation.

Nearly all the 16 pages of Eysenck's rejoinder to Kamin are taken up, not with point-by-point answers to his criticisms as would be expected in a scientific debate, but in a many-times-over repetition of Kamin's faults as he sees them: Kamin is behaving as an adversary rather than as a seeker after truth (p. 157); his work is 'absolutely vague', containing 'different and incompatible criticism' (p. 161), and 'cannot be trusted to be factually accurate' (p. 165). He characterizes Kamin's criticism of the tests used by Shields as 'derogatory remarks (that) are factually incorrect and motivated perhaps by a desire to impugn, by suggestion, a research project the results of which are difficult to account for in terms of a purely environmentalistic hypothesis' (p. 165). Even if Eysenck sincerely thought this he gained nothing by voicing his suspicions of Kamin's integrity. It seems incongruous that he should accuse Kamin (p. 157) of abusing his adversary. The result is that Eysenck leaves himself no time to refute the erroneous assumptions, suppressions of the truth and deliberate misrepresentations that he sees in Kamin's work. The early studies upon which he based his own case he sees as scientific, and important in their own time (p. 158) despite their faults. Consequently, despite Kamin's criticisms, he is confident that 'the genetic hypothesis remains essentially unscathed' (p. 171).

Summing up

The reader must expect of me a personal assessment of the outcome of the debate, and it would be fainthearted of me to withhold it. My view is that Kamin has succeeded in destroying the credibility of Eysenck's bases for the quantitative estimation of heritability, namely the studies of twins reared apart, on account of the incompleteness of their separation; the environmental similarity of each twin-pair; correlation of IQ with age and tester-bias; studies of MZ/DZ twin-pairs and siblings on account of their divergence from genetic prediction, perhaps due to a tendency to treat children who look and behave alike more similarly and the effects of this on mental development; kinship studies on account of extremely variable correlations and more recent findings which do not support the genetic-model; adoption studies on account of selective placement, restricted variance and the inconsistency of the correlations obtained in recent research; sex linkage, because the genetic hypothesis generally fails to find confirmation; inbreeding depression, because of the confusion with socioeconomic and city/rural status; reaction times, because of lack of published evidence; EEG evoked potentials because the evidence is contradictory and on balance negative.

In awarding this verdict I must remind readers of the meaning of the term heritability: it is a measure of the proportion of the variability in a trait – in the present instance that of 'intelligence' as measured by IQ – that can be attributed to genetic factors. Heritability has to do solely with the variation found within a given population. It is not an estimate of the extent to which genetic or environmental influences determine a trait. For example, in a genetically homogeneous strain of laboratory rats heritability, as a measure of variation, would be near zero. Heritability has likewise nothing to do with the differences in genetic constitution which serve to differentiate humans from chimpanzees. To say, therefore, that we have not the evidence on which to base estimates of heritability within a given human population is not to deny a genetic conditioning for human characteristics, including behaviour. If, therefore, it be conceded, as in my view it must be, that we have no reliable empirical bases for the calculation of heritability even within a given population, we do not have to fall back upon a hypothesis of purely environmental determination. Kamin has not demonstrated any such as regards IQ differences, and indeed did not set out to do so. He was merely exercised to show that the findings of the various studies quoted as evidence of a mainly genetic determination could be interpreted as resulting from environmental differences. My own view is that while he, especially in the studies of twins, has demonstrated an environmental contamination which destroys their value for the calculation of heritability, he has not satisfactorily accounted for the whole of the greater resemblance in IQ found in MZ twins as opposed to ordinary sibling. Hence we cannot deny that genetic differences may play some part in the observed differences in people's mental capabilities. But the complexity of successive gene–gene and gene–environment interactions – with the possibility that any one of them can set the individual's development on a new course in which a different array of genes becomes effective within a different environment – will for ever nullify attempts to calculate the 'contributions' of heredity and environment by a mathematical model. On this question of heredity and environment we are reduced to a position of indeterminacy akin to that of the physicist in trying to predict which atoms will collide with each other. It could even be argued that the concept of a quantitative heritability has no validity beyond a particular individual, since to strike an average where individual variation must be so large produces a meaningless statistic.

The value of the debate, as I see it, is that it has exposed the fruitlessness of the search for the determinants of 'intelligence' and of academic ability in terms of separable genetic versus environmental 'contributions'. It has removed a compulsion from our minds which has misdirected research effort over two generations like some alchemist's search for the means of making gold. Twin and adoption studies can no longer be seen, simplistically, as natural experiments in apportioning the roles of nature and nurture. It is not a question of bigger and better studies. We shall never be able to place twins from birth in separate environments randomized in a manner that meets the canons of scientific acceptability. Likewise we shall never be able to find adopted children whose true mothers have life-histories typical of the population as a whole, nor could the children be placed with randomly selected foster-mothers. If these sampling problems do not deter the would-be researcher, let him or her realize that the results of any such utopian study would have little generality. Meticulously controlled studies of animal learning have come up with only one general conclusion: there is no such thing as a general superiority of learning-ability: the strain of animals who do best in one test sometimes do worst in another (Fuller and Thompson 1978, pp. 135–51). One might even postulate genetic safeguards against too much excellence (which indeed would be lethal in a natural population because it would destroy the food supply). The idea that there is a bundle of dominant genes uniformly making for high IQ would imply that the human species is genetically unique in an unlikely way. It must have been just as necessary to control the competence of early human beings as it has been to control the aggressiveness or sexual prowess of rats and mice. The notion of the 'contributions' of a personified heredity or environment has more affinity with the church offertory box than with empirical studies of how genes affect development.

Once it is recognized that in searching for means of apportioning the 'contributions' of heredity and environment researchers have been following a will-o'-the-wisp that leads them into a scientific morass, the way will be cleared for more attainable research objectives. Up to the present time comparatively little time and money has been spent on the study of early human development. (cf. B. L. White 1977, p. 346 – 'Experimental studies of the effects of early experiences that last longer than an hour or so have rarely been performed with human infants'). And the only large-scale follow-up study of prenatal effects (Broman *et al.* 1975) missed all the most important, i.e. the exteroceptive influences, owing to the neglect of animal studies of crowding and harassment (Ader and Belfer 1962; Bruce 1960; Chitty 1952; Thompson 1957; summarized in Stott 1962) and of exploratory retrospective studies of the effects of pregnancy stress in humans (Stott 1957, 1961).

Table 1

Comparison of correlations for IQ found for 1. one twin of a DZ pair and a sibling, and 2. DZ twins.

Authors of the studies	Sibling–DZ twin	DZ twins
Snider (1955)	0.26	0.32
Stocks and Karn (1933)	0.12	0.65
Partanen et al. (1966) (two samples)	0.41 0.34	0.51
Huntley (1966)	0.58	0.58
Reed and Reed (1965)	0.34	0.60

The first four are taken from Kamin (1974), the fifth from Fulker (1975).

Table 2

	Adopted child and adoptive midparent	Own child and adoptive midparent	Control child and true midparent	Adopted child and adoptive midparent having own child
Freeman et al.	0.39 (169)	0.35 (28)		0.18 (25)
Burks	0.20 (174)		0.52 (100)	
Leahy	0.18 (177)	0.36 (20)	0.60 (173)	
Pooled data	0.26 (520)	0.35 (48)	0.57 (273)	0.18 (26)

The numbers are given in brackets.

References

ADER, R. and BELFER, M. L. (1962). 'Prenatal maternal anxiety and off-spring emotionality in the rat, *Psychol. Rep.*, **10**, 711–8.

BASHI, J. (1977). 'Effects of inbreeding on cognitive performance', *Nature*, **266**, 440–2.

BAYLEY, N. and SCHAEFER, E. S. (1966). 'Correlations of maternal and child behaviors with the development of mental abilities'. Data from the Berkeley Growth Study. *Monographs of the Society for Research in Child Development*, **29**, (6, Serial No. 97).

BLATT, B. and GARFUNKEL, F. (1969). *The educability intelligence: Pre-school intervention with disadvantaged children*. Washington D.C. Council for Exceptional Children.

BROMAN, S. H., NICHOLS, P. L. and KENNEDY, W. A. (1975). *Preschool IQ: Prenatal and Early Development Correlates*. Hillsdale, New Jersey: Erlbaum.

BRUCE, H. M. and PARROTT, D. M. V. (1960). 'Role of olfactory sense in pregnancy block by strange males', *Science*, **131**, 1526.

BURKS, B. S. (1928). 'The relative influence of nature and nurture upon mental development: A comparative study of foster parent-foster child resemblance and true parent-true child resemblance', *Yearbook of the National Society for the Study of Education* (Part 1), **27**, 219–316.

BURT, C. (1955). 'The evidence for the concept of intelligence', *British Journal of Educational Psychology*, **25**, 158–77.

CASPARI, E. W. (1977). 'Genetic mechanisms and behaviour' In: OLIVERIO, A. *Genetics, environment and intelligence*. Amsterdam, New York, Oxford: North-Holland.

CHITTY, D. H. (1952). 'Mortality among voles (microtus agrestis) at Lake Vyrwy, Montgomeryshire in 1936–39', *Phil. Trans. Soc. London, B.*, **236**, 505–52.

DAVIE, R., BUTLER, N. R. and GOLDSTEIN, N. (1972). *From Birth to Seven* Second Report of the National Child Development Study. London: Longman and National Children's Bureau.

DeFRIES, J. C., JOHNSON, R. C., KUSE, A. R., McLEARN, G. E., POLOVINA, J.,

VANDENBERG, S. G. and WILSON, J. R. (1979). Familial resemblance for specific cognitive abilities', *Behavior Genetics*, **9**, 23–43.

DENENBERG, V. H. (1977). 'Interactional effects in early experience research'. In: OLIVERIO, A. *Genetics, environment and intelligence.* Amsterdam, New York, Oxford: North-Holland.

DOBZHANSKY, T. (1962). *Mankind evolving.* New Haven: Yale University Press.

DOBZHANSKY, T. (1973). *Genetic diversity and human equality.* New York: Basic Books.

ERLENMEYER–KIMLING, L. and JARVIK, L. F. (1963). 'Genetics and intelligence: a review', *Science*, **142**, 1477–9.

ERTL, J. and SCHAFER, E. W. P. (1969). 'Brain response correlates of psychometric intelligence', *Nature*, **223**, 421–2.

EYSENCK, H. J. (1979). *The Structure and Measurement of Intelligence.* New York: Springer-Verlag.

EYSENCK, H. J. and KAMIN, L. (1981). *Intelligence: The Battle for the Mind.* London and Sydney: Pan Books.

FIRKOWSKA, A., OSTROWSKA, A., SOKOLOWSKA, M., STEIN, Z., SUSSER, M. and WALD, I. (1978). 'Cognitive development and social policy', *Science*, **200**, 1357–62.

FREEMAN, F. N., HOLZINGER, K. J. and MITCHELL, B. C. (1928). 'The influence of environment on the intelligence, school achievement and conduct of foster children', *Yearbook of the National Society for the Study of Education* (Part 1), **27**, 103–205.

FULKER, D. W. (1975). 'Review of The Science and Politics of IQ, by L. J. Kamin', *American Journal of Psychology*, **88**, 505–19.

FULLER, J. L. and THOMPSON, W. R. (1978). *Foundations of behaviour genetics.* St. Louis, Missouri: Mosby.

GUTTMAN, R. (1974). 'Genetic analyses of analytical spatial ability: Raven's Progressive Matrices', *Behavior Genetics*, **4**, 273–83.

HERRMAN, L. and HOGBEN, L. (1932). 'The intellectual resemblance of twins', *Proceedings of the Royal Society of Edinburgh*, **53**, 105–29.

HILDRETH, G. H. (1925). *The Resemblance of Siblings in Intelligence and Achievement.* New York: Teachers College, Columbia University.

HORN, J. M., LOEHLIN, J. C. and WILLERMAN, L. (1979). 'Intellectual resemblance among adoptive and biological relatives: The Texas Adoption Project', *Behavior Genetics*, **9**, 177–207.

HUNTLEY, R. M. C. (1966). 'Heritability of intelligence'. In: MEADE, J. E. and PARKES, A. S. (Eds) *Genetic and Environmental Factors in Human Ability.* New York: Plenum.

HUTCHINGS, B. and MEDNICK, S. A. (1977). 'Criminality in adoptees and their adoptive and biological parents: A pilot study. In MEDNICK, S. A. and CHRISTIANSEN, K. O. (Eds) *Biosocial Bases of Criminal Behavior*, Chapter 7. New York: Gardner Press, pp. 127–41.

JENSEN, A. R. (1980). *Bias in mental testing.* New York: Free Press.

JUEL-NIELSEN, N. (1965). 'Individual and environment: a psychiatric-psychological investigation of monozygous twins reared apart', *Acta Psychiatrica et Neurologica Scandinavica* (Monograph Supplement 183).

54   Reference

KAMIN, L. J. (1974). *The Science and Politics of IQ*. Potomac, Maryland: Erlbaum.

KAMIN, L. (1981). *See* Eysenck, H. J. and Kamin, L. (1981).

LAWRENCE, E. M. (1931). 'An investigation into the relation between intelligence and inheritance', *British Journal of Psychology* (Monograph Supplement 5).

LEAHY, A. (1935) 'Nature-nurture and intelligence', *Genetic Psychology Monographs*, **17**, 241–306.

LEHRKE, R. G. (1978) 'Sex linkage: a biological basis for greater male variability in intelligence'. In OSBORNE, R. T., NOBLE, C. E. and WEYL, N. (Eds). *Human Variation: The Biopsychology of Age, Race and Sex*. New York: Academic Press.

LOEHLIN, J. C., and NICHOLS, R. C. (1976) *Heredity, Environment and Personality*. Austin: University of Texas Press.

NEWMAN, H. H., FREEMAN, F. N. and HOLZINGER, K. J. (1937) *Twins: A Study of Heredity and Environment*. Chicago: University of Chicago Press.

NICHOLS, R. C. (1965) 'The inheritance of general and specific ability', *National Merit Scholarship Research Reports*, **1**, 1–9.

OUTHIT, M. C. (1933). 'A study of the resemblance of parents and children in general intelligence', *Archives of Psychology*, No. 149.

OVERSTREET, H. A. (1926). '*Influencing human behavior*'. New York: Norton.

RECORD, R. G., McKEOWN, T. and EDWARDS, J. H. (1969). 'The relation of measured intelligence to birth weight and duration of gestation', *Annals of Human Genetics*, **33**, 71–9.

REED, E. and REED, S. (1965). *Mental Retardation: A Family Study*. Philadelphia: Saunders, p. 77.

RUST, J. (1975). 'Cortical evoked potential, personality and intelligence', *Journal of Comparative and Physiological Psychology*, **89**, 1220–6.

SCARR, S. (1980). *Race, Social Class and Individual Differences*. Hillsdale, New Jersey: Erlbaum.

SCARR, S. and WEINBERG, R. A. (1978). 'The influence of "family background" on intellectual attainment: The unique contribution of adoption studies', *American Sociological Review*, **43**, 674–92.

SCHIFF, M., DYME, M., DUMARET, A., STEWART, J., TOMKIEWICS, S. and FEINGOLD, J. (1978). 'Intellectual status of working-class children adopted early into upper middle-class families', *Science*, **200**, 1503–4.

SCHULL, W. J. and NEEL, J. V. (1965). *The Effects of Inbreeding on Japanese Children*. New York: Harper and Row.

SHIELDS, J. (1962). *Monozygotic Twins Brought up Apart and Brought up Together*. London: Oxford University Press.

SKODAK, M. and SKEELS, H. (1949). 'A final follow-up study of one hundred adopted children', *Journal of Genetic Psychology*, **75**, 85–125.

SMART, J. L. (1977). 'Early life malnutrition and later learning ability: A critical analysis'. In: OLIVERIO, A. *Genetics, environment and intelligence*. Amsterdam. New York, Oxford: North-Holland.

SPUHLER, K. P. (1976). Family resemblance for cognitive performance: An assessment of genetic and environmental contributions to variation. Unpublished doctoral dissertation, University of Colorado.

STOTT, D. H. (1957). 'Physical and mental handicaps following a disturbed pregnancy', *Lancet*, i, May 18, 1006–12.

STOTT, D. H. (1960). 'Interaction of Heredity and Environment in regard to "Measured Intelligence"', *British Journal of Educational Psychology*, **30**, 95–102.

STOTT, D. H. (1961). 'Mongolism related to emotional shock in early pregnancy', *Vita Humana*, **4**, 57–76.

STOTT, D. H. (1961). 'An empirical approach to motivation based on the behaviour of a young child', *Journal of Child Psychology and Psychiatry*, **2**, 97–117.

STOTT, D. H. (1962). 'Cultural and natural checks to population growth' In: MONTAGU, M. F. A. (Ed) *Culture and the Evolution of Man*. New York: Oxford University Press. Reprinted in: VAYDA, A. P. (Ed) (1969). *Environment and Cultural Behavior*. American Source Books in Anthropology. Nat. History Press.

STOTT, D. H. (1973). 'A follow-up study from birth of the outcome of different prenatal stresses', *Developmental Medicine and Child Neurology*, **15**, 770–87.

STOTT, D. H., MARSTON, N. C. and NEILL, S. J. (1975). *Taxonomy of Behaviour Disturbance*. (USA and Canada) Ontario: Brook Educational (UK and Australia) London: Hodder and Stoughton.

STOTT, D. H. and LATCHFORD, S. A. (1976). 'Prenatal antecedents of child health, development and behaviour; an epidemiological report of incidence and association', *Journal of the American Academy of Child Psychiatry*, **15**, 161–91.

STOTT, D. H. (1978). *The Hard-to-Teach Child* University Park Press; (UK and Australia) London: Ward Lock Educational. (Published in the UK by Ward Lock under the title: *Helping Children with Learning Difficulties*.)

STOTT, D. H. (1981). 'Behaviour disturbance and failure to learn: A study of cause and effect', *Educational Research*, **23**, 163–72.

TABAH, L. and SUTTER, J. (1954). 'Le niveau intellectuel des enfants d'une même famille', *Annals of Human Genetics*, **19**, 120–50.

THOMPSON, W. R. (1957). 'Influence of prenatal maternal anxiety on emotionality in young rats', *Science*, **125**, 698–9.